Pat Mc

A Taste of the West Country

A collection of original recipes created by
Taste of the West award-winning chefs and producers

wemakemagazines

A catalogue record for this book is available
from the British Library.

ISBN 978-0-9933352-0-4

Published by We Make Magazines Ltd
wemakemagazines.co.uk

Editor: Jennie Cooper
Sub-editor: Deborah Martin
Designer: Jeff Cooper

Thanks to Belinda Berwick and Emma Grainger
and the rest of the team at Taste of the West; also
to Maria Griffen

Contents

Foreword

You can't go too far in this part of the world without being struck by the beauty of the rolling countryside or entranced by the miles of coastline. Verdant fields, clear waters, happy herds and passionate, knowledgeable people are the key ingredients of our thriving food and drink industry.

Furthermore, an appetite-whetting selection of farm shops, delis, restaurants and foodie events such as cookery courses and festivals, all use and help promote the home-grown produce and talent found in abundance across the West Country.

So, how best to celebrate the region's food and drink? Our answer: by devising a blend of award-winning chefs and producers from Taste of the West to create this special recipe book, *A Taste of the West Country*.

Why is our book different? We wanted to create a keepsake that celebrates the people and produce behind our region's wonderful food and drink scene, and have focused on the Taste of the West's award winners. We paired chefs and producers from across Cornwall, Devon, Dorset, Somerset, Gloucestershire and Wiltshire to create original recipes that can be prepared at home. Some are elaborate, others simple and straightforward; all are delicious.

What better way to get a genuine Taste of the West Country? We hope you enjoy cooking these dishes.

John Sheaves
Chief Executive, Taste of the West

All recipes serve 4

Gloucestershire

Elderflower and Bramley & Gage 6 o'clock Gin
panna cotta, lemon sorbet and ginger crumb   10

Martin's Meats lamb T-bone and fresh coconut makhani   14

Elderflower and Bramley & Gage 6 o'clock Gin panna cotta, lemon sorbet and ginger crumb

Recipe by Martin Adams, Head Chef, Tudor Farmhouse, Clearwell

For the panna cotta
2½ gelatine leaves
300ml double cream
70ml milk
140ml Bramley & Gage 6 o'clock Gin
80g sugar
3-4 elderflower tops

For the lemon sorbet
Zest of 4 lemons
600ml water
600g sugar
300ml lemon juice
50g glucose

For the ginger crumb
75g salted butter
75g sugar
190g flour
20g ground ginger

To make the panna cotta
1   Soak the gelatine in cold water for five minutes.
2   Bring the milk, cream and sugar to the boil, simmer for 2½ minutes, then take off the heat and add the gin.
3   Add the elderflower tops and leave for 20 minutes to allow the flavour to infuse. Remove the flower tops.
4   Add the gelatine, stir, then pass through a sieve.
5   Pour the liquid equally into four dario moulds and refrigerate until firm.

To make the lemon sorbet
1   Bring the water and sugar to the boil, simmer for two minutes, then add the lemon juice and zest.
2   Cool to room temperature, then churn in an ice cream machine and freeze. Alternatively, place in a shallow bowl in the freezer and break with a fork every 30 minutes until it sets.

To make the ginger crumb
1   In a bowl mix all the ingredients until it has a sand-like texture.
2   Place on a baking tray and bake at 180°C/gas mark 4 for 15-20mins, or until golden brown. Cool to room temperature.

To serve
1   Turn out the panna cotta by placing the moulds in hot water for 10 seconds, then tip onto a plate.
2   Spoon some of the crumb around the panna cotta and place a scoop of sorbet on the crumb.

Martin Adams, Head Chef, Tudor Farmhouse, Clearwell

"My inspiration for this recipe came from Bramley & Gage's 6 o'clock Gin, plus the abundance of elderflower in our garden at the Tudor Farmhouse. One important factor when cooking this dish is to make sure the elderflower is young.

My favourite ingredient would have to be wild garlic – it's free, organic and has such a wonderful flavour. I would urge anyone when sourcing any ingredient to use the best possible producers, preferably local to you.

The best part of my job is that I get to work with food, which is what I love. I wouldn't say there were any worst parts – I just love it all!

When I am not in the kitchen I enjoy fly fishing on the River Wye, which is just down the road from the restaurant at Redbrook. I also love running through the forest."

Michæl Kain, Managing Director, Bramley & Gage, Thornbury

"Our second-generation family distillery produces gins and liqueurs. The business grew out of farm diversification. Some 25 years ago my parents owned a soft-fruit farm and Dad started making liqueurs with the surplus fruit.

As our skills grew, I set out to make a top-quality London dry gin (a style of gin, not a geographical denomination). To do this, I had custom-made a hand-beaten copper 'double bubble' still.

The variety of the fruit in our products is very important. Not all varieties of strawberries taste the same; 'Elsanta' may be bomb-proof but it just doesn't pack the flavour of some of the older varieties like 'Cambridge Favourite'. The fruit's ripeness also makes a huge difference. The same goes for the botanicals in our gin: fully ripe junipers taste so much better.

My favourite part of the job is sitting in a comfy armchair at six o'clock for a moment of 'ginspiration'. The worst is emptying the still – distilled elderflowers form a sort of glue-like substance!"

Martin's Meats lamb T-bone and fresh coconut makhani

Recipe by Shamsul & Monrusha Krori,
The Curry Corner, Cheltenham

Ingredients

4 lamb T-bones (170-200g each)
100g fresh coconut
2 tbsp ground almonds
6 whole Kashmiri chillis, dried
6 plump garlic cloves, finely chopped
2.5-cm piece of ginger, peeled and
   finely chopped
1 tsp turmeric powder
1 tsp coriander powder
1 tsp cumin powder
1 tsp Kashmiri chilli powder
2 tejpata bay leaves
10-cm piece of cinnamon stick
4 green cardamoms
1 black cardamom
2 cloves
½ tsp cumin seeds
½ tsp fennel seeds
½ tsp mustard seeds
1 tbsp pure ghee
2 large onions, chopped
3 medium tomatoes, finely chopped
8 fresh curry leaves
3 tbsp fresh coriander
Cornish sea salt to taste
1 tsp sugar
2 tbsp fresh local cream
Pinch of saffron

Method

1. Crack a fresh coconut and remove the flesh. Peel off the brown skin left on the flesh with a potato peeler. Cut the flesh into small pieces and put in a grinder. Grind until coarse in texture. Put aside.
2. Heat the ghee in a saucepan on medium heat and fry the onion until golden brown. Add the garlic and ginger, then the curry leaves, then the powdered spices and then the fresh spices. Add a little water (about 4 tablespoons) and cook for about 15 minutes until the flavours are released. (The spices and other ingredients must be added in the specific order given.) Work quickly, stirring vigorously, as the ingredients must not burn or overcook.
3. Add the almonds, then the lamb, stirring regularly.
4. Next add the tomatoes, fresh coconut, fresh coriander and sugar and cook for another 5 minutes. Add salt to taste.
5. Add 800ml of water, then the saffron, and cook, covered, until the meat is done (about 1 hour).
6. Just before serving add the cream.
7. Serve with fresh saffron pilau rice and homemade organic naan.

"When you cook, put your heart and soul into it; it sounds like a cliché, but it's true. Love makes food taste truly delicious."

Monrusha Krori

Shamsul and Monrusha Krori, Chefs/Patrons, The Curry Corner, Cheltenham

Run by this father and daughter team, The Curry Corner was opened by Shamsul in 1977. He started cooking at the age of 16, inspired by his mother's authentic traditional cooking and her insistence on flavour and perfection. He has passed on those values to his daughter, who left a career as a barrister to pursue her passion for cooking good food.

Their work is inspired by tradition, but their innovative techniques result in a sophisticated layering of flavours. Every morning they prepare fresh spices, which they fuse with the finest fresh local produce. Among their favourite ingredients are saffron handpicked from Morocco, plump fiery-red Kashmiri chillies and fresh coconut. This recipe for lamb makhani was created by Shamsul in 1977 and is still served in the restaurant. Fragrant and aromatic, it balances so many ingredients yet the hero of the dish remains the local lamb. It's not surprising that Shamsul is called the Spice Master!

Their cooking has been praised by Gordon Ramsay and by Michael Palin, who described it as 'the best curry from pole to pole'.

Wiltshire

Royal Bassett Blue cheese beignets, caramelised pear,
walnut pastry, petit salad, sweet and sour dressing   20

Arkell's Bee's Organic Ale & honey-poached nectarines,
filled with a sweet cinnamon mascarpone   24

Wiltshire Chilli Farm Chipotle Chilli Salt gravadlax   30

Royal Bassett Blue cheese beignets, caramelised pear, walnut pastry, petit salad, sweet and sour dressing

Recipe by Russell Hunt, Head Chef, Marsh Farm Hotel, Royal Wootton Bassett

For the beignets
140ml full-fat milk
70g unsalted butter
115g plain flour
4 large eggs
1 tsp chopped rosemary
120g Royal Bassett Blue cheese
Sea salt to taste

For the caramelised pear
75g castor sugar
1 star anise
500ml water
1 firm pear

For the walnut pastry
50g crushed toasted walnuts
2 sheets feuille de brick pastry
25g butter

For the dressing
75ml sherry vinegar
1 tsp clear honey
1 tsp Dijon mustard
Sea salt
Ground pepper
200ml rapeseed or olive oil

25g mixed baby leaf salad to garnish

To make the beignets
1 In a thick-bottomed saucepan melt together the butter and milk.
2 Sift in the flour and whisk together until the mixture begins to form a dough and stick to the side of the pan.
3 Whisk in the blue cheese and transfer to a mixing bowl.
4 Add the eggs, one at a time and beat until the mixture has formed into a smooth dough, then add the chopped rosemary, check the seasoning and set aside to cool.
5 To finish, pre-heat a deep fryer to 160/170° degrees and use a dessertspoon dipped in hot water to spoon the mixture carefully into the fryer. (You will need two or three beignets to make one portion.) Gently fry for 4 minutes until golden brown, rotating all the time.

To make the caramelised pear
1 Place 50g of the sugar in a small pan with 500ml of water and the star anise. Bring to the boil until the sugar has dissolved, then reduce the heat.
2 Cut the pear into cubes roughly 1.5cm in size and add to the syrup.
3 Gently poach for 5-10 minutes, or until the pear is just cooked. Remove from the heat, then place the pear cubes on a piece of kitchen towel to dry. Set aside.
4 Before serving, dust the pear with the remaining castor sugar, then, using a kitchen blowtorch, you can caramelise the sugar to give the fruit a beautiful sweet crunch.

Continued on page 23...

To make the pastry

1 Gently melt the butter, then lightly brush each sheet of pastry and press together.
2 Sprinkle with the walnuts and bake in a preheated oven at 170°/gas mark 3 for around nine minutes, or until golden brown.
3 Leave to cool then break into shards for texture.

To make the dressing

1 Place the sherry vinegar, mustard and honey in a mixing bowl and whisk together.
2 Slowly add the oil, continually whisking until the dressing emulsifies. Check the seasoning

To serve

Arrange the beignets, caramelised pear cubes and pastry shards on plates and garnish with salad leaves and dressing. Serve as a starter.

"This recipe uses classic combinations prepared in an interesting way, and is packed with flavour and texture. It's a simple thing to do well, to impress your family and friends."

Russell Hunt, Marsh Farm Hotel

Ceri Cryer, Brinkworth Dairy, Hill End Farm, Brinkworth, Chippenham

"My husband, Chad, and I run this traditional, welfare-friendly dairy farm, producing milk, yoghurt, cream, butter, ice cream, cheese and honey. We own a Brinkworth pedigree Friesian herd (established in 1910) to make all our dairy products. We supply to shops, pubs, restaurants and farmers' markets in Wiltshire, Gloucestershire, London and further afield.

Royal Bassett Blue was the cheese I wanted to develop when we first started, and we have now perfected it. It won its first award in 2014 for Best Cheese at the Taste of the West Awards.

Running a dairy farm is not without peril. We once had a scary moment rescuing a cow from a brook. The vet gave it coffee to revive it afterwards!

Our dairy has a wonderful view of the Dauntsey Vale, so the motivation for why we are doing this (to preserve the landscape) is right in front of us. The worst aspect is caring so much, it's hard to stop working!"

Arkell's Bee's Organic Ale & honey-poached nectarines, filled with a sweet cinnamon mascarpone

Recipe by Eilsley Haynes, Head Chef at Arkell's Brewery pub, The Saracen's Head in Highworth

Ingredients

1 vanilla pod
500ml bottle of Arkell's Bee's Organic Ale
200g demerara sugar
3 tbsp organic honey
4 firm nectarines, halved with stones removed
100g mascarpone
4 tbsp icing sugar
Pinch of cinnamon

Method

1 Split the vanilla pod lengthwise and scrape out the seeds. Put them and the pod into a saucepan (large enough to hold the fruit), then add the ale, sugar and honey and bring this gently to a boil, stirring occasionally to ensure the sugar dissolves.

2 Reduce the heat, add the nectarines and top with enough water to cover them.

3 Poach the fruit gently for about 12-15 minutes (depending on the fruit's firmness), turning halfway, until the fruit is tender when pierced with a sharp knife. Remove and place in a bowl.

4 Increase the heat and boil the poaching liquid until it has reduced by two-thirds and is a syrupy consistency.

5 Allow the syrup to cool, then pour it over the fruit and chill until ready to serve.

6 Thoroughly mix the mascarpone with all the icing sugar and a pinch of cinnamon.

7 Place the nectarines in dishes with a little syrup, and fill each with a small scoop of the flavoured mascarpone, decorate with a spring of fresh mint and serve... Beerlicious!

Eilsley Haynes, Head Chef, Arkell's Brewery pub
The Saracen's Head, Highworth

"I have created this flavoursome nectarine dish poached in our Organic Ale, as the nectarine absorbs the sweetness of the organic honey, one of the main ingredients in the beer.

Inspired by my mum, I became a chef in 1975 and I love traditional cooking. Having trained at Blunsdon House Hotel in Swindon, I rose to the rank of Head Chef there, and have worked for Arkell's Brewery since 1999 in almost a dozen of the brewery's 100 pubs across the south of England.

I believe a good meal should be full of flavour and value for money. If you've got both those, you've got a great meal. Personally, I love a good steak and kidney pie, roast lamb, or fish – anything really, as long the dish doesn't contain broad beans! I can't stand them! I also dislike okra, I've tried them both once, but would never do so willingly again."

Alex Arkell, Arkell's Brewery, Stratton St Margaret

"I am a sixth-generation family member, Head Brewer, and known as 'beer supremo' at Arkell's Brewery. We brew a range of different beer styles in cask, bottle and keg, which are sold mainly in Wiltshire, Gloucestershire, Oxfordshire, Berkshire and Hampshire.

My top tip for matching food with beer is to consider the balance and intensity of flavour. Choose bitterness with spiciness, or maltiness with sweetness. In my experience, any food with any beer will always be pretty good, so don't be scared to give it a try.

The best part of my job is watching people's reactions to new recipes I've created; the worst is when these are bad reactions, which is obviously very rare! My proudest moment in brewing so far was winning gold at The Society of Independent Brewers' National Beer Awards for our 1843 Lager, a recipe I'm very proud of."

Wiltshire Chilli Farm Chipotle Chilli Salt gravadlax

Recipe by Aron Davies, Head Chef, The Swan Inn, Wilton, Marlborough

Ingredients

2 salmon fillets, approx 500g each
50g sea salt
75g castor sugar
Wiltshire Chilli Farm Chipotle Chilli Salt
Handful of fresh chopped coriander
Shot of vodka (optional)
1 lime

Note: the curing process needs to be started 48 hours ahead of required serving time.

Method

1   Check the salmon for bones by running your fingers along the surface of the flesh.
2   Mix together the sugar, sea salt and coriander (and vodka if using).
3   Lie a large piece of cling-film on the work surface, big enough to wrap both fillets when they are placed on top of one another.
4   Sprinkle about a quarter of the sugar/salt mix on to the cling-film, then place the fillets side by side, skin side down on top of the mixture.
5   Liberally grind the Chilli Salt over the salmon.
6   Now use two-thirds of the remaining sugar/salt mix and sprinkle it over the first fillet. Then place the second fillet on top of the first, so that sugar/salt mix is sandwiched between the pink flesh and the skin is uppermost.
7   Sprinkle the remaining sugar/salt mix over the skin of the second fillet, squeeze them together and wrap them tightly in the cling-film. Then wrap the entire parcel in another layer of cling-film.
8   Put the fish parcel in a container or tray and then place a similar-sized container or tray on top. Add some tins or weights on the top of this and place in the fridge for 48 hours, turning once during the this curing time.
9   Unwrap in a sink – you will be astounded how much liquid has come out of the fish, which should now be nice and firm. Dry it with a kitchen towel.

To serve

Either dice the fish or slice it diagonally so that the marinade is left on one outside edge. Serve on top of a mixed salad with a squeeze of lemon or lime and a dense brown bread.

"Never take a bath (after handling extreme peppers) – that just turns you into chilli soup!"

Martin Bond

Aron Davies, Head Chef, The Swan Inn, Wilton, Marlborough

"At The Swan Inn we like to keep food simple and let the ingredients speak for themselves. The Wiltshire Chilli Farm Chipotle Chilli Salt is a fantastic and versatile product. It is brilliant for seasoning meat, especially steaks before grilling them. We also use it to season the batter for our cod and chips (delicious) and we have tried using it to make salt and pepper squid (equally delicious)!

In the end we chose this recipe because it will be easy to re-create at home. Use the best and freshest salmon you can find. Try sniffing it: this sounds odd, but it shouldn't smell too fishy and the flesh should be nice and tight, oily to the touch and not slimy."

Martin Bond, Owner/Director, Wiltshire Chilli Farm, Whitley, near Melksham

"My colleagues Jamie Sythes, Kevin Gover, Simon Morgan and I are owners/directors of Wiltshire Chilli Farm. We grow chillies to use in our award-winning sauces, jams, salts and snack products.

I love the travelling aspect of my job. It's great to see new faces at anything from a local farmers' market to a big food festival, enjoying what we craft for the first time. Working with the extreme peppers is by far the most challenging aspect: I love to eat them, but I don't love washing the pans after cooking them! As a rule of thumb we always say that the best way to get rid of the "I'm holding a ball of fire" effect is '48 hours and four showers'. Never take a bath – that just turns you into chilli soup!

I enjoy challenging my tastebuds to hotter and hotter sauces, although I still haven't managed a teaspoon of our God Slayer!"

Somerset

Slow-cooked belly of pork with Perry's Cider
and a sage and cider gravy   36

Brown Cow Organic Vanilla Yoghurt & cardamom
caramelised rice pudding with spiced rhubarb compote   40

Beech Ridge Farm free-range chicken,
mushroom and bacon hotpot gratin   44

Old Spot pork tenderloin with Heavenly Hedgerows
Three Fruit Marmalade and a cider sauce   46

Asparagus with Waddling Free duck
eggs, pancetta and black garlic   50

Pan-fried fillet of Cornish hake with a Lyme Bay
crab, saffron, spinach and pea risotto using Keen's
Whey Butter, with pea shoots and garlic oil   56

Beech Ridge Farm duck with orange, sesame seeds,
sweet potato and green beans   60

Apple and cider rarebit with Langsford's
Bread and Butter Pickle   64

Slow-cooked belly of pork with Perry's Cider and a sage and cider gravy

Recipe by Jane Bond, Chef/Proprietor, New Farm Restaurant, Over Stratton

Ingredients

2 Bramley apples, diced
1 leek, roughly chopped
2 garlic cloves, smashed
Sprig of fresh sage
500ml Perry's Dabinett Cider
1l chicken stock
1.2kg piece scored boneless pork belly (Ask your butcher to remove all the bone from the pork.)

Top Tip: Perry's single variety Dabinett Cider makes an ideal accompaniment to this dish

Method

1 The first stage is best done the day before to make removing the excess fat easier. Put all the ingredients except the pork into a casserole dish or deep baking tray, then place the meat on top and season with salt and pepper. The pork should be totally submerged – if it isn't, top up with water. Cover the dish with a lid or tent of foil and place it in the oven for three hours at 180°C/gas mark 4.

2 Once the pork is cooked, leave it to cool slightly in the stock then carefully lift it onto a tray, discarding any tiny pieces of vegetables or herbs, then leave to cool in the fridge overnight. Put all the cooking juices, apple and vegetables into a jug or small saucepan, cover and chill.

3 The following day place the pork on a board. With a sharp knife, carefully cut the skin off the meat, then cut it into four equal squares. Crisp this up in a hot oven (220°C) ready to be served with the pork. Trim any excess fat off the meat, which again should be cut into four equal squares, and set aside until ready to cook.

4 Add any of the braising juices left (they may now be jelly) to the saucepan containing the cooking juices. You could use a hand-blender to make a naturally thickened gravy.

5 Place the pork pieces in a lidded casserole dish, splash a bit of cider in the bottom, put the lid on tight and place in a pre-heated oven 180°C/gas mark 4 for 20-30 minutes.

6 Heat up the gravy, adding more liquid (cider!) if necessary, and warm the crisped skin for five minutes, before removing the pork from the oven.

7 Serve the pork on mashed potato with stir-fried curly kale. Top with the crisp crackling and pour a generous amount of the cider gravy around.

"We are surrounded by orchards so naturally a lot of my inspiration is Somerset based and cider features strongly"

Jane Bond

Jane Bond, Chef/Proprietor, New Farm Restaurant, Over Stratton

"I am lucky enough to have been born and bred in Somerset. It is a wonderful county — when I am out in the orchards walking our dog on a sunny day, there is nowhere better.

When not working in the kitchen you can usually find me out in the garden, either tending the flowerbeds or in the vegetable patch where we grow produce for ourselves and for the restaurant.

Our restaurant is my granfie's old farm and we are surrounded by orchards so naturally a lot of my inspiration is Somerset based and cider features strongly. It goes well with everything and is as good as or even better than wine to enhance the flavours of dishes. I use it with chicken, fish, game and of course one of my favourites, pork.

One of the biggest joys of running a restaurant is the appreciation of your food by the customers, and this dish always gets a great reception."

George Perry, Managing Director and Cider Maker, Perry's Cider, Dowlish Wake

"We produce craft ciders from our own grown apples and surrounding orchards. As well as supplying throughout the UK, we export to Europe and even Japan.

The best part of being a cider maker for an independent company is the freedom to produce ciders that we want to make. It's also really great to be involved in the whole process from the orchard to the bottle.

The most exciting time of year is the beginning of the harvest, when we first get to look at the year's crop and are able to get an idea of what the vintage is going to be like.

One of our company's greatest achievements is winning Supreme Cider Champion three times in six years at the British Cider Championships. However, living just 200 yards from the cider works, it can be hard to switch off. I do a lot of cycling and running, though, for which the surrounding Somerset landscape is ideal."

Brown Cow Organic Vanilla Yoghurt & cardamom caramelised rice pudding with spiced rhubarb compote

Recipe by Rebecca Owen, Head Chef, The Lordleaze Hotel, Chard

For the rice pudding
1.2l West Country milk
100g pudding rice
120g castor sugar
1 large bay leaf
5 green cardamom pods, bashed
300g Brown Cow Organics Live
    Vanilla Yoghurt, lightly whipped

For the compote
400g rhubarb, cut into 2cm batons
3 balls of stem ginger, grated
500ml stock syrup
A pinch of freshly ground black
    pepper

Top Tip: This can all be prepared ahead and keeps for up to four days in the fridge. Leave the bruléeing until the last minute. If you have any left over, it is also delicious for breakfast with dried fruit and granola

To make the rice pudding
1   Put the bay leaf, milk, cardamom and sugar into a pan and bring to the boil. Allow to cool for 30 minutes to infuse.
2   Pour the milk mixture through a sieve, retaining all of the infused milk.
3   Pour the milk back into a heavy-bottomed pan and bring gently to the boil.
4   Add the rice and reduce the heat to a gentle simmer. Cook for 1 hour, stirring frequently. Allow the mixture to cool and refrigerate for at least an hour.
5   When ready to serve, loosen the rice pudding with a fork and then fold in the Brown Cow Vanilla Yoghurt until well combined.
6   Place the rice pudding mixture into serving rings or ramekins. Brulée the surface of the puddings by adding castor sugar and place under a very hot grill for a few minutes.

To make the compote
1   Bring the stock syrup to the boil, then add the rhubarb and reduce heat to a simmer.
2   Cook for 4 minutes, then add the black pepper and ginger.
3   Strain off the liquid through a sieve and retain the spiced fruit.
4   Serve alongside the rice puddings.

Judith Freane, Brown Cow Organics, Pilton, Shepton Mallet

"I took over the Guernsey dairy herd in the late 1990s from my father, and started producing yoghurt in the early 2000s on Perridge Farm. A total of four farms make up our 480 organic acres.

At Perridge Farm we breed and raise our Guernsey dairy cows to produce milk for yoghurts. Any surplus is sent to the Organic Milk Suppliers Co-operative. We also produce award-winning organic beef from our male bulls, plus a range of interior and fashion items from the cow hides.

Herd nutrition is paramount to us. We analyse every field's soil and crops and monitor the herd's diet. A small team produces our organic yoghurt — a naturally thick, rich yoghurt without thickeners, artificial colours, additives or preservatives.

Running my farm and business is a way of life. The beauty of our farm inspires me every day and it's important that every aspect of our business is ethical, with the utmost care taken of our cows."

Beech Ridge Farm free-range chicken, mushroom and bacon hotpot gratin

Recipe by Rebecca Owen, Head Chef, The Lordleaze Hotel, Chard

Ingredients

4 breasts of Beech Ridge Farm free-range chicken, cut into 2cm-wide strips
6 rashers of back bacon, diced
3 banana shallots, diced
75g butter
3 tbsp olive oil
10 closed-cup mushrooms, quartered
300ml dry white wine
300ml good chicken stock
500ml West Country double cream
½ tbsp dried tarragon
2 cloves of fresh garlic, crushed
500g Cheddar cheese, grated

Method

1 Heat the oil in a large pan on a medium to high heat, then add the chicken. Cook for 2 minutes each side to seal, then remove and set aside.
2 Add the butter and another splash of oil to the pan, then add the shallots, garlic and bacon and sauté for 5 minutes. Add the mushrooms and sauté for another 5 minutes.
3 Increase the heat to maximum and add the wine and tarragon. Reduce by two-thirds.
4 Add the stock and reduce again by two-thirds.
5 When the mixture is reduced and aromatic, add the cream and the chicken plus any resting juices. Reduce the heat to a simmer and cook for 15 minutes.
6 Transfer to a serving dish or heat-proof bowls, top with the cheese and put under a preheated hot grill to brown before serving.

"Mushroom and bacon hotpot has been a constant on our menu, and the addition of this delicious chicken makes a great main course to share, with crusty bread and a crisp salad."

Old Spot pork tenderloin with Heavenly Hedgerows Three Fruit Marmalade and a cider sauce

Recipe by Simon Barrington-Jones, Truffles Brasserie, Bruton

For the pork

800g Kimbers' Old Spot pork tenderloin

400g Kimbers' Old Spot pork sausage, skin removed

250g Kimbers' Old Spot smoked sliced back bacon, rind removed

1 tbsp Heavenly Hedgerows Three Fruit Marmalade

Sea salt and freshly ground black pepper

1 tsp vegetable oil

For the sauce

37.5cl bottle Pilton keeved cider

285ml chicken stock

Local honey to taste

Method

1 Heat the oven to 190°C/gas mark 3.

2 Cut a slash down the pork loin to form a pocket down its length. Take the sausage and stuff it into the pocket.

3 Spread a piece of aluminium foil onto the work surface and lay on the rashers of bacon to form a rectangular sheet of meat. Lay the stuffed loin onto the bacon, at right angles to the rashers, and spread the marmalade on top of the pork. Season with sea salt and black pepper, then roll up using the foil to help you make a tidy roll.

4 Now carefully roll out of the foil onto an oiled baking tray, with the loose ends of the bacon tucked underneath the roll.

5 Heat the vegetable oil in an ovenproof frying pan, then place the roll join side down into the hot fat to seal the join. Gently turn the roll and fry until the bacon starts to colour.

6 Return to the baking tray and place in the oven for 20-25 minutes. Remove from the oven and set aside to rest for at least 10 minutes.

7 Meanwhile, make the sauce. Place the cider and chicken stock in a saucepan and reduce on a low heat until syrupy. Add honey, but retaining some of the tartness of the cider, and season to taste, then set aside.

8 To serve, slice the pork and arrange on a bed of braised root vegetables, with buttery mash and steamed runner beans. Pour over the sauce and garnish with a few thyme and chive flowers.

Simon Barrington-Jones, Truffles Brasserie, Bruton, Somerset

"The inspiration for this recipe comes from the ingredients. There are many variations on this dish, but this one shows off the character of the beautiful Old Spot pork that Kimbers produces. The Heavenly Hedgerows marmalade adds the perfect citrus tang without overwhelming the flavour of the meat. The sauce is very simple because the traditional Pilton keeved cider has such a natural taste it is important not to mask it with other flavours; just ensure you use a well-flavoured, good-quality stock and don't season it until after it has reduced. I have used Kimbers meats for over 20 years, and through Taste of the West have come to know the other producers that make working in this part of the county such a privilege.

After 35 years of cooking, my top tip is to buy the best quality ingredients you can; it is better to spend your budget on shin of beef from an award-winning farmer than it will ever be to buy fillet steak from an anonymous source. Happy cooking!"

Asparagus with Blackacre Farm's Waddling Free duck eggs, pancetta and black garlic

Recipe by Brett Sutton, Chef/Owner, The White Post, Rimpton

Ingredients

16 spears of asparagus

8 long rashers of thinly cut Capreolus pancetta, cut in half

4 Waddling Free free-range duck eggs from Blackacre Farm

3 cloves of black garlic

Handful of edible flowers (such as chive flowers, nasturtiums, three-cornered garlic, marigolds and so on)

Cornish sea salt and cracked black pepper

Rapeseed oil

Method

1 Preheat the oven to 180°C/gas mark 4.

2 Cook the eggs – we use Waddling Free as the yolks are vivid yellow but better still they taste amazing and are very rich. These are popped into a water bath at 62°C for 1 hour.

3 For the asparagus, trim off the base of the stem where it appears to become woody and cook in boiling salted water for 2 minutes. Then plunge into iced water, drain and dry well.

4 Wrap each asparagus spear in the pancetta and place on a baking tray. Cook in the oven for 6-7 minutes.

5 Crush the black garlic with the back of a knife to make a paste.

To serve

Smear the black garlic paste evenly on four plates. Place the pancetta-wrapped asparagus on this, then place an egg next to each serving. Season the egg with the black pepper and sea salt. Add a few edible flowers and a drizzle of rapeseed oil.

Top Tip: This recipe works with poached or soft boiled eggs too, but I recommend investing in a water bath. If you have a thermometer, and can find a cool spot on your oven top, that also does the trick!

Briony Wood, Farmer, Blackacre Farm Eggs, North Cheriton

"Blackacre is home to some very content girls of the clucking, quacking and chirping variety! We produce what we consider to be the best free-range hen, duck and quail eggs in the business. Working with independent retailers, restaurants and hotels across the South West, plus dabbling with a few in London, we have been producing eggs for more than 35 years on our farm in Somerset, and are planning on being around for at least double that again with the help of the next generations of egg collectors!

We are very lucky to have worked with Brett and Kelly Sutton from The White Post Restaurant in Rimpton over the last few years, and are so pleased that Brett is creating a recipe using our duck eggs. A family favourite, our three little 'uns love making their own puddings with Brett after Sunday lunch!"

Pan-fried fillet of Cornish hake with a Lyme Bay crab, saffron, spinach and pea risotto using Keen's Whey Butter, with pea shoots and garlic oil

Recipe by Nick Hampson, Head Chef, Bocabar Glastonbury, and Janey Syrett, Head Chef, Bocabar Bristol

Ingredients

4 Cornish hake fillets, each 200-225g
200g hand-picked Lyme
    Bay white crab meat
300g arborio risotto rice
2 small banana shallots, finely diced
1 small garlic clove, finely diced
Drizzle of rapeseed oil
150ml white wine
900ml vegetable stock
90g Keen's Whey Butter
200g peas, lightly blanched
200g spinach, lightly blanched
1 punnet pea shoots
1g saffron strands
Sea salt (for the hake)
Salt and pepper (for the risotto)
Drizzle of garlic oil

Method

1   Preheat the oven to 180°C/gas mark 4.
2   Place a large-based saucepan on a medium heat, add a drizzle of rapeseed oil and lightly fry the shallots and garlic. Add the rice and stir, slowly adding the vegetable stock, little by little.
3   Add the saffron, white wine and half the whey butter. Simmer for around 8-10 minutes on a low heat until the rice becomes slightly soft.
4   While the rice is simmering, fry the hake fillets in a non-stick pan, skin-side down, for a couple of minutes until lightly golden brown. Add the remaining whey butter, turn the hake over, season with Cornish sea salt and place in the oven for 6 minutes.
5   Once the rice is cooked, fold in the peas, spinach and crab and season.
6   To serve, place the hake on top of the risotto, finish with pea shoots and a drizzle of garlic oil.

Top Tip: When making this dish, don't overcook the risotto – you don't want to end up with a mushy mess on the plate. Keep stirring the risotto and checking how quickly it is cooking. Always make sure the fish has a crispy skin.

Nick Hampson, Head Chef, Bocabar Glastonbury and Janey Syrett, Head Chef, Bocabar Bristol

"We both love seafood, especially from the south coast, and this is a very popular dish in both restaurants that represents the best fish in the country (in our opinion)!

We love using saffron; it has a vibrant colour and adds a lovely flavour to dishes.

The best part of the job is being able to be creative with the great local produce from our suppliers.

A proud moment since working at Bocabar for Nick was gaining the Gold Award from Taste of the West within six months of opening. A proud moment for Janey has been winning Best Café Food Award at the Bristol Good Food Awards, as well as the Gold Award from Taste of the West."

George Keen, Keen's Cheddar, Wincanton

"The Keen family have been making unpasteurised cheddar since we moved to Moorhayes Farm in Wincanton in 1899. Five generations later, we are still thriving.

Whey butter has been made since mechanical cream separators were developed by Dr Lister. The small amount of cream in the cheddar whey makes a tasty butter, if you have the patience to assemble and clean the separator; there are 96 discs to clean, so it's an opportunity to contemplate the world's problems while involved in the task!

Keen's milk makes curds for champion cheddar and the whey left has a small quantity of cream to make prize-winning butter. The cheese-making process adds flavour to the butter, which will enhance any recipe. Butter is the original spread and it's interesting to see customers returning to the comforting smooth taste of butter on bread or biscuits."

Beech Ridge Farm duck with orange, sesame seeds, sweet potato and green beans

Recipe by Christopher Cleghorn, Head Chef, Olive Tree Restaurant at The Queensberry Hotel, Bath

Ingredients

4 Beech Ridge Farm duck breasts
2 large sweet potatoes
300g coarse sea salt
3 organic oranges
300g green beans
20g sesame seeds, toasted
10g sesame oil
10g honey (good quality)
2g Chinese allspice

Method

1 Spread the sea salt on a flat tray and place the sweet potatoes on top. Cook in a preheated oven at 180°C/gas mark 4 for 1 hour, turning after 25 minutes. Once cooked, scoop out the flesh and blend until smooth. Season and reserve till needed.

2 Lightly score the duck breasts, following the natural lines. Pan fry with enough oil to just cover the layer of fat until golden brown – approx. 5-8 minutes over a medium heat. (The oil is just to render the existing fat out.)

3 Once the skin is crisp, strain off the oil, turn and cook for 3 minutes on each side. Remove from heat and brush with a little honey and a sprinkle of Chinese spice. (The duck can be cooked earlier to make sure it is well rested.)

4 Peel the oranges using a straight knife to remove all the white pith. Reserve the segments in their own juice.

5 Remove the black tip of the green beans with a knife and blanch in lightly salted boiling water for 2 minutes. For best results serve straight away, finishing them with the sesame oil and toasted sesame seeds.

6 Warm the duck at 180°C/gas mark 4 for 3 minutes before serving.

7 To serve, swipe the sweet potato puree over the plates, add the green beans, then the duck breast sliced in half, followed by the orange segments.

Top Tip: Make sure that while cooking the duck you give it 100 per cent attention, to avoid overcooking it.

Christopher Cleghorn,
Head Chef,
Olive Tree Restaurant at
The Queensberry Hotel, Bath

"The inspiration for the recipe came from our philosophy on food. We use best quality, seasonal and fresh ingredients to emphasise the flavour of the food without overpowering it.

The best part of my job has to be using the incredible products from the season and always striving to be better every day. The worst part is when you start as a chef, making sure you take the time to learn as much as possible on how to cook each ingredient. It is worth it, however, because this allows you to create each element in a dish, maximising the flavour to its best. My top general cooking tip would be always buy seasonal and local because the quality difference can be dramatic."

Chris Dibble and Hollie Stamp,
Beech Ridge Farm, Wellington

"We started Beech Ridge Farm in 2009, as I (Chris) had always loved working with poultry. I have come from a long line of farmers and my parents own a large dairy farm in Devon.

I started breeding geese as a young child and enjoyed it so much that I ventured on to breed chickens, ducks and turkeys. The farm started out as two empty fields, but has now become established as a respectable fully fledged, free-range poultry farm. We farm chickens, ducks, bronze turkeys, guinea fowl and geese.

I slaughter all our own produce on site, and process it on site in our butchery department. It is then prepared by hand to ensure good care and quality.

We are very proud of how much we have achieved from what started out as so little. We now produce 'from field to folk' and this is, without doubt, our greatest achievement."

Apple and cider rarebit with Langsford's Bread and Butter Pickle

Recipe by Nigel Bissett, Head Chef, Swan Hotel, Bristol

Ingredients

225g mature farmhouse cheddar cheese, grated

2 eating apples, cored and thinly sliced

25g butter

25g plain flour

2 tsp wholegrain mustard

50ml dry cider

Cayenne pepper to taste

4 slices of bread

Langsford's Bread and Butter Pickle

Method

1 Preheat the grill.

2 Melt the butter in a saucepan and mix in the flour, cooking on a medium heat for two minutes.

3 Whisk in the cider and cheese, stirring until melted to make the rarebit.

4 Add the mustard and cayenne pepper, and when fully mixed remove from the heat and leave to cool.

5 Toast one side of your bread under the grill and on the other spread the pickle and top with slices of apple.

6 Roll out the rarebit between two sheets of baking paper and place on top of the apple. Place under the grill until it bubbles and turns golden brown.

7 To serve, cut the rarebit into triangles, add some crispy leaves and enjoy with the rest of the bottle of cider.

Top Tip: Organisation! Get everything prepared and to hand, then you are ready to cook and watch the results.

"I chose this recipe because, like all my creations, it is simply what I enjoy to eat. When you consider this dish, think of it as a platform from which to spark your own ideas."

"We have a fair division of labour: I cook, my husband lugs it all around, and my girls eat as many samples as they can before they get caught – perfect!"

Dawn Langsford,
Langsfords Preserves, Bath

"I started making preserves as a hobby because I love cooking. Gradually my hobby has developed into a thriving family business. We have a fair division of labour: I cook, my husband lugs it all around, and my girls eat as many samples as they can before they get caught – perfect!

A highlight of my job is the people I meet at the markets and food festivals we attend. The worst part is the vinegar fumes that we all absorb and wear like a fine fragrance during chutney season!

While I don't take myself too seriously, I am serious about good food. I care about what goes into my products, how they are made and how they taste. It was one of my proudest moments when I received my first Gold Taste of the West award in 2013. I (very modestly) rang everyone I had ever met!"

Dorset

Local watercress, homemade chorizo, garlic
croutons and a poached egg salad   70

Fillet of sea bass, with a celeriac and wasabi remoulade, potato
terrine, asparagus and a lemon and lime mayonnaise   74

Fillet of brill with wild garlic, flageolet beans with guanciale, scallops
wrapped in lardo, Capreolus Fine Foods' Capreolus Coppa   78

Toasted brioche with smoked mutton,
wild garlic and Francis cheese   80

Wild garlic and guanciale with bouchee   80

Roast asparagus wrapped in Capreolus
Fine Foods' Coppa from Dorset   82

Smoked mackerel pâté   88

Cumin and Coriander Olive fougasse bread,
Olive Oil and Red Chilli Harissa houmous   90

Seared scallops, with an avocado rillette and sauce vièrge,
using Dorset Farms' Honey Smoked Streaky Bacon   94

Local watercress, homemade chorizo, garlic croutons and a poached egg salad

Recipe by Emma Smith, Head Chef and Landlady,
The George Inn, Chideock

For the chorizo
500g pork mince
10g salt
19g paprika
5g fennel seeds
1 garlic clove, minced
5 tbsp red wine
2g cayenne pepper

For the croutons
2 garlic cloves, minced
3 tbsp olive oil
2 slices of stale bread, diced
Pinch of salt

For the salad and dressing
1 tsp Dijon mustard
1 tsp honey
2 tbsp extra virgin olive oil
2 tbsp white wine vinegar
Bunch of watercress
Four eggs

Top Tip: make sure the individual elements of the dish are properly prepared before putting them together

To make the chorizo
1   This is best made a day or two in advance. Put all ingredients in a bowl and mix thoroughly.
2   The mixture can be stored for up to six days in a sealed container in the fridge.

To make the croutons
1   Preheat oven to 150°C/gas mark 2. Mix together the garlic, salt and oil. Place the diced bread on a tray, drizzle the garlic oil over it and toss to coat. Spread out in a single layer.
2   Bake for 15 minutes, then set aside.

To make the salad
1   Whisk all the dressing ingredients in a bowl, then set aside.
2   Bring a pan of water to the boil then allow to simmer.
3   Meanwhile, add a splash of oil to a frying pan and when hot, crumble in the chorizo mixture. Cook without turning for one minute, then turn and cook until brown for another minute.
4   Set the chorizo aside and cover with foil to keep warm.
5   Wash and drain the watercress, then pour over the dressing.
6   Crack the eggs into four separate cups, add a dash of vinegar to the simmering water and stir to create a gentle whirlpool. Slowly tip the eggs in one at a time. Cook for three minutes, then remove with a slotted spoon and drain on kitchen paper.

Continued on page 73...

7 While the eggs are cooking, place the dressed watercress onto plates, top with the cooked chorizo and sprinkle on the garlic croutons. Finally top with the poached eggs and serve.

"This dish as a sort of deconstruction of our very popular Chideock Scotch Egg made with chorizo that is featured on our pub menu."

Emma Smith, The George Inn, Chideock

Tom Amery, Managing Director, The Watercress Company, Dorchester

"My family have been farming watercress in Dorset and Hampshire since the 1860s. Our watercress is grown in purpose-built, gravel-lined beds, fed with mineral-rich spring water, one of the reasons the crop is so naturally high in calcium.

Our organic, 'longer lasting' crop is hand-harvested, complete with roots, and will keep far longer in the fridge than the cut crop. It lends itself to a wide range of recipes.

One of the most rewarding parts of my job is exploring new markets and uses for our product. As well as soups, sandwiches and sauces, we now supply watercress for use as a culinary powder that goes into chocolate, ice creams and even in gin.

As well as growing this crop, our company also produces a range of baby leaf salad and has most recently launched The Wasabi Company."

Fillet of sea bass, with a celeriac and wasabi remoulade, potato terrine, asparagus and a lemon and lime mayonnaise

Recipe by Tony Shaw, Head Chef, Riverside Restaurant, West Bay

Ingredients
800g sea bass
250g asparagus

For the remoulade
1 medium-sized celeriac, cut into thin
   strips
50g spring onions, finely sliced
50g coriander, finely chopped
25g freshly grated wasabi from The
   Wasabi Company
150g peeled brown shrimps
150g white crab meat
50g mini capers

For the potato terrine
8 large potatoes, peeled
250g unsalted butter
Salt and pepper

For the lemon and lime mayonnaise
2 egg yolks
1 tsp white wine vinegar
1 tsp Dijon mustard
½l olive oil
1 lemon, zest and juice
1 lime, zest and juice
Salt and pepper

To make the potato terrine
1   Make the terrine the day before. Line a dish with cling film, thinly slice the potatoes by using a mandolin, then layer in the dish, sandwiching each layer with the butter and seasoning, until the dish is full.
2   Cook at 180°C/gas mark 4 for one hour, then cool in the fridge overnight.
3   The next day, slice the terrine into four portion sizes and cook at 180°C/gas mark 4 for five minutes before serving.

To make the lemon and lime mayonnaise
1   In a bowl, whisk the egg yolks, vinegar and mustard, then slowly add the oil until a nice thick consistency is reached. If it's too thick, add a little hot water.
2   Season and, keeping half the mayonnaise aside for the remoulade, add to the remainder the zest and juice of the lemon and lime for the dressing.

To make the remoulade
Place all the ingredients in a bowl and mix together with the reserved mayonnaise.

To cook the sea bass and asparagus
1   Heat 1 tsp of olive oil in a non-stick frying pan. Season the fish, place skin side down and cook for 4 minutes. Turn over and cook for a further 2 minutes.

Continued on page 77...

2 While cooking the fish, blanch the asparagus in salted, boiling water for 3 minutes, then drain.

To serve
Place the seabass on top of the asparagus spears, with the remoulade and a portion of potato terrine alongside. Drizzle the mayonnaise dressing around the dish.

Tony Shaw, Head Chef, Riverside Restaurant, West Bay

"I have worked at the Riverside for the past eight years and was promoted to Head Chef four years ago. I am passionate about cooking with seasonal, local produce and creating dishes that excite the palate.

I like being inventive, so enjoyed the challenge of incorporating locally grown wasabi into one of my dishes – a product I have not used fresh before. I chose sea bass as I felt the wasabi would bring out its flavour, and I'm very pleased with the result. When cooking this dish, use the wasabi as soon as it is grated to give maximum flavour to the dish. Don't overcook the fish: it needs your full attention.

It's a privilege to be able to produce dishes from ingredients I have on my doorstep, in particular sourcing fresh fish and shellfish from Lyme Bay and serving it in the restaurant within a few hours."

Jon Old, Manager, The Wasabi Company, Dorchester

"Our company grows fresh wasabi in Dorset and Hampshire, and supplies it nationwide to the UK, as well as to Europe and occasionally beyond.

The wasabi plant is 100% edible, so we sell the leaves, leaf stems, flowers and the all-important rhizomes that are grated to make fresh paste. It is traditionally paired with sushi, but more chefs are finding new ways to use wasabi, as in this delicious-looking dish from The Riverside.

Wasabi takes at least 18 months to reach maturity, so it's a patient man's game waiting for harvest. Our first harvest was a memorable occasion. Although no one had tried fresh wasabi before, we knew we were onto something as soon as the aromatic, sweet and earthy pungency hit our taste buds. I'm still trying new ways to enjoy fresh wasabi. My latest obsession is serving it with the cheeseboard; it goes spectacularly well with blue cheese."

Fillet of brill with wild garlic, flageolet beans with guanciale, scallops wrapped in lardo, Capreolus Coppa

Recipe by Ian Simpson, Chef/Proprietor, The White House, Charmouth

Ingredients

4 120g brill fillets
50ml fish stock
A generous couple of handfuls of wild garlic (spinach can be substituted if wild garlic isn't in season)
12 hand-dived scallops
12 thin slices of lardo
300g flageolet beans
150g guanciale, chopped
4 large or 8 small slices of Capreolus Coppa (thinly sliced cured shoulder of pork)
300g unsalted butter
Zest and juice of one lemon
Splash of vegetable oil

Method

1 If you are making a fish stock, prepare this in advance and reduce it so it has thickened.
2 Wrap the scallops in the lardo and keep to one side.
3 Fry the chopped guanciale in a little butter, add the flageolet beans and season with a little black pepper. Keep warm to one side.
4 Fry the Coppa in a little vegetable oil over a steady heat so that it crisps. Place on some paper to drain.
5 In a small saucepan, heat the lemon zest and half the lemon juice with a little of the fish stock. Take off the heat and whisk in 200g of the softened butter. Put to one side in a warm place.
6 Dust the brill with flour and fry in the remaining butter and a glug of oil until golden brown and just cooked. Keep warm to one side.
7 In the same pan, sear the scallops for one minute on each side until golden brown. Remove and keep warm.
8 Finally, in the same pan quickly fry the wild garlic so that it starts to wilt: it won't take long!

To serve

1 Assemble the dish with the beans at the bottom, then some wild garlic, then the cooked fish on top. Finally, place the scallops around the plate and the crisp Coppa on top.
2 Drizzle the butter sauce around the dish, and garnish with a little finely shredded wild garlic.

Toasted brioche with smoked mutton, wild garlic and Francis cheese

Recipe by Ian Simpson, Head Chef, White House Hotel, Charmouth

Ingredients

8 slices of toasted brioche, cut into pieces about 2.5x5cm
4 slices Capreolus' Smoked Mutton
4 wild garlic leaves
4 thin slices Francis cheese

Method

1 Place the slices of mutton on a board. On each place a wild garlic leaf, then a slice of the cheese.
2 Wrap the cheese with the garlic and the mutton. (I use a cheese like Francis because it is punchy enough to stand up to the already punchy flavours of the wild garlic and the mutton.)
3 Place onto the toasted brioche, cut each in half and serve

Wild garlic and guanciale with bouchee

Recipe by Ian Simpson, Head Chef, White House Hotel, Charmouth

Ingredients

8 pre-cooked bouchee (small pastry shell) cases
1 egg
50g wild garlic leaves
50ml double cream
50g Capreolus' guanciale (cured pig cheek)
Ground black pepper

Method

1 Blend the egg, cream and wild garlic into a smooth puree to make a wild garlic custard and season with black pepper (the guanciale is salty enough).
2 Dice the guanciale, fry in a little oil for one minute, drain, then place into the bouchee cases, and pour in the wild garlic custard to fill them.
3 Bake in the oven at 170°/gas mark 3 for 3-4 minutes until set.

Roast asparagus wrapped in Capreolus Fine Foods' Coppa from Dorset

Recipe by Ian Simpson, Head Chef, White House Hotel, Charmouth

Ingredients
8 asparagus spears
8 slices of Capreolus Coppa
Splash of olive oil

Method
1 Remove any woody part of the asparagus stalks, then steam for one minute by placing about an inch of water in a pan, putting a lid on and steaming over a moderate heat. Don't add too much water: you need to create steam rather than boil the asparagus.
2 Refresh in cold water.
3 Pat dry, then drizzle with olive oil.
4 Roll two spears in each slice of the Coppa, place on a baking tray and roast in the oven at 190°C/gas mark 5 for two minutes.

> "Accept the fact that sometimes things don't turn out exactly like the photo in the book, and improvise when you have the confidence to."
>
> Ian Simpson

Ian Simpson, Chef/Proprietor, The White House, Charmouth

"The inspiration for my brill dish came from spring flavours, the produce from the sea on our doorstep and the quality produce that Capreolus sends our way. When preparing it, be careful with the seasoning. The cured parts of the dish, such as the lardo, pig's cheek and Coppa, are already salted.

A cooking tip to share is that most recipes should be viewed as a guide. Accept the fact that sometimes things don't turn out exactly like the photo in the book, and improvise when you have the confidence to. Try changing some of the ingredients if you can't source everything as per the recipe.

Ingredients-wise, I always love April when the wild garlic starts to grow like mad in all the fields and valleys behind our village. I love to go foraging on a spring day; but do hold on to your keys – I once dropped mine in a copse dense with wild garlic, and it took me two hours to find them!"

Karen and David Richards, Capreolus Fine Foods, Rampisham

"Capreolus Fine Foods is an artisan charcuterie producer, owned and run by ourselves since 2009 when we started our business.

Our range includes traditional pork products and we also make charcuterie from beef, venison, mutton, duck, chicken and goat. We work very closely with local farmers to ensure that we are using meat that has been raised to the highest husbandry standards – free-range is our minimum requirement.

We supply all over the country to numerous restaurants, exhibit at far too many food festivals, and also sell online. Our proudest moment was when our Guanciale was named Taste of the West Champion Product in 2013.

When we are not working I (Karen) unwind in the garden, as I'm a very keen gardener, while David either walks the dog or occasionally goes shooting at Bisley."

Smoked mackerel pâté

Recipe by John Kellas, Owner and Cook,
Aroma Coffee House & Kitchen, Lyme Regis

Ingredients

200g smoked mackerel, skins
  removed
300g full fat soft cheese
1 lemon, zest & juice
1 tbsp wholegrain mustard
1 tbsp horseradish (slightly less if using
  freshly grated)
Good pinch of pepper

Top Tip: When cooking this dish, do
not add any salt, and remember to
remove the fish skins before blitzing!
If you would like to add a bit of colour,
then include some finely chopped dill.

Method

Put all the ingredients into a food processor and blitz until
you've achieved the required texture. That's it!

This simple recipe takes only a couple of minutes to make
and doesn't involve any cooking, so no excuses!

"I've always liked fish pâté, and with all
the tourist mackerel fishing trips leaving
from the Cobb, there is a nice link."

Cumin and Coriander Olive fougasse bread, Olive Oil and Red Chilli Harissa houmous

Recipe by Matt Street, Head Chef, The Eastbury Hotel, Sherborne

For the bread

1kg of T55 Shipton Mill Flour
600g water at 20°C
20g salt
25g fresh yeast
150g Olives Et Al Moorish Cumin and
   Coriander Olives

For the houmous

1 400g can chickpeas, drained and
   rinsed
5 tbsp Olives Et Al Olive Oil
1 garlic clove, crushed
2 tbsp Olive Et Al Red Chilli Harissa
   Paste
1 tbsp tomato puree
1 lemon or lime

Method

1 Combine the yeast and water and leave for 10 minutes. Then add this to the flour and salt to make the dough. Leave covered for 1½ hours in a warm place.
2 Pull out the dough and shape 150g pieces into triangles. Roll out and cut slits in the bread with a sharp knife or dough cutter. Push in the pitted olives all over the dough.
3 Allow the bread to prove again on a tray, covered with a bag, for 40 minutes. Meanwhile, make the houmous.
4 Put the chickpeas, olive oil, crushed garlic, harissa paste and tomato puree, along with a couple of pinches of salt, into a blender. Blitz this up with a squeeze of lemon or lime, then put straight into your favourite serving dish. Add a generous dollop of harissa paste and drizzle olive oil over the top.
5 Set the oven to 200°C/gas mark 6 and put a roasting tin in the bottom. Remove the bread from the bag and place the tray in the oven, then put 100ml of water into the roasting tin; this will add moisture while the bread is cooking, which will add colour to the bread. Bake for 15-20 minutes.
6 Grab a sharing plate or board and put on it the freshly baked fougasse bread, the bowl of harissa houmous and a small dipping dish of olive oil as a further dip for your warm beautiful bread.

Matt Street, Head Chef,
The Eastbury Hotel, Sherborne

"This recipe can be easily made at home; it is suitable as a quick, light meal or a great addition to a charcuterie dinner. Once the bread dough is finished and baking in the oven, the rest is all about enjoyment.

My favourite ingredients are all types of pepper, from capsicum to naga chilli, as there are so many uses for them in all cuisines.

The best part of my job is being able to create amazing and exciting things for people; the worst part is not having enough time in the day to do it for yourself! My most exciting and nervous time was in 2009 when I competed in the Roux scholarship competition and the BBC Masterchef Professionals series; both were new experiences for me.

To unwind, I usually like to travel to the coast and experience new restaurants with good company."

Seared scallops, with an avocado rillette and sauce vièrge, using Dorset Farms' Honey Smoked Streaky Bacon

Recipe by Steve Pielesz, Head Chef, Beaminster Brasserie
at the BridgeHouse Hotel, Beaminster

Ingredients

12 scallops, with roe on
4 rashers of Dorset Farms' Honey
    Smoked Streaky Bacon
2 ripe avocados, diced
2 shallots, finely diced
1 small red chilli, seeded and sliced
3 lemons
2 vine tomatoes, seeded and diced
1 bunch of flat-leaved parsley, finely
    chopped
1 clove of garlic, finely chopped
1 tbsp baby capers
100g butter
100ml olive oil
Pea shoots to garnish

To make the avocado rillette

1   Dice the avocados. Add one shallot, the chilli and the juice of one lemon.
2   Lightly mix together, adding salt and pepper to taste.

To make the sauce vièrge

1   Combine the tomatoes, one shallot and the garlic with the olive oil.
2   Add the zest of one lemon, then segment the fruit and chop it into the mix, along with the parsley.
3   Mix in the capers and chill.

To cook the bacon

1   Preheat oven to 175°C/gas mark 3.
2   Lie the bacon rashers between two flat roasting trays and bake in the oven for 15 minutes or until crispy.
3   Remove from the oven and cool on a rack.

To cook the scallops

1   Season the scallops and place in a hot frying pan with 1 tsp of olive oil for approximately 30 seconds.
2   Add the butter. When it foams, add the juice of a lemon.
3   Remove from the heat and turn the scallops: they are ready to serve.

Top Tip: Do not turn, shake or move the scallops when cooking.

Continued on page 97...

To serve

1 Place three spoonfuls of the rillette onto each plate, then the scallops on top.
2 Add a generous spoonful of the sauce vierge around the plate and drizzle a small amount of the scallop butter.
3 Finally, arrange the bacon on the plate and garnish with the pea shoots.

Sarah Chaffey, Sales & Distribution Manager, Dorset Farms, Littlewindsor

"I have worked at Dorset Farms since I was asked to do a delivery for them 25 years ago! I'm still here. Why? Because I love my job and I sell the best bacon around. When I started, we were a pig-rearing unit. Now I market award-winning bacon and ham throughout the UK. Not bad for a company most delivery drivers can't even find.

Our success, reflected in the number of awards on my office wall, has come from a constant determination by the whole workforce to produce the best possible product using only organic and free-range West Country pork. We brine cure our bacon and you won't find any milky residue or shrinkage when you cook it.

I often get new samples to try (another reason why I love my job!), but don't take my word for it — try it for yourselves."

Devon

Chicken breast, buffalo mozzarella, sun-ripened tomatoes, wrapped in Denhay Dry-cured Back Bacon

Recipe by Ian Middleton, Head Chef at Dukes in Sidmouth

Ingredients

4 chicken breasts
8 slices of Denhay Dry-cured Back Bacon
2 buffalo mozzarella balls, drained and sliced
8 halves of sun-ripened tomatoes
1 bunch of spring onions, finely chopped
6 large maris piper potatoes, peeled and chopped
Pinch of salt and pepper
Knob of butter
Oil for frying

Method

1 Preheat the oven to 200°C/gas mark 6. Make a pocket in each chicken breast by slicing one side of them (not all the way through). Stuff each pocket with sliced mozzarella and two sun-ripened tomatoes.

2 Wrap each chicken breast in two slices of bacon, making sure the ends of the bacon sit underneath the chicken.

3 Put them on a tray lined with greaseproof paper, drizzle with a little olive oil. Cook for 25-30 minutes, until the juices run clear.

4 Cook the potatoes until soft, mash, then add butter, salt and pepper.

5 Pan fry the chopped spring onions until soft, then add to the mashed potato, and serve.

"I created this recipe as it is similar to a dish we have done in the past at Dukes that was always a big seller."

> "The pork is hand-rubbed in sea salt and is given time to slowly mature, resulting in a bacon that is wonderfully succulent and is undoubtedly all about flavour."

Jim Loescher, Managing Director, Denhay, Honiton

"Denhay produces award-winning traditional bacon from a bespoke factory in Honiton, using British outdoor-reared high-welfare pork. The pork is hand-rubbed in sea salt and is given time to slowly mature, resulting in a bacon that is wonderfully succulent and is undoubtedly all about flavour.

Although we no longer farm pigs, having developed this craft of curing the finest bacon means that we are able to continue to produce dry-cured bacon. Our brands – Denhay and Spoiltpig – both emphasise that the pork used is from RSPCA Freedom Food-assured farms. Sourcing high-welfare British meat is an essential part of the business and one that helps us stand out from our competitors.

Denhay has been farming in the Marshwood Vale in Dorset since 1952. Today we farm nearly 2,000 acres and continue to milk 1,000 cows from our four herds."

Double-baked pressed pork belly, using Bell & Loxton Cold Pressed Rapeseed Oil

Recipe by James Chapman, Executive Head Chef,
Victoria Inn, Salcombe

Ingredients
1kg pork belly, boned and scored
300ml Bell & Loxton Cold Pressed
    Rapeseed Oil
Cracked black pepper
Salt
Fresh thyme

Method
1   Place the pork belly (skin side up) in a deep roasting tray or casserole dish.
2   Pour the oil all over it until the meat is sitting in half its height in oil. Season liberally with salt and cracked black pepper, rub the thyme over the top and place remaining stalk in the surrounding liquor.
3   Roast at 150°C/gas mark 2 for approximately 1½ hours.
4   Remove the pork from the roasting dish, wrap in greaseproof paper and transfer it to another container.
5   Place something flat on the top and weigh it down with a couple of kilo weights (you could use bags of sugar or flour or even a saucepan filled with water). Once cooled, refrigerate for at least three hours; overnight would be preferable.
6   Remove the paper, plus any excess fat and jelly that has formed, trim any unsightly edges and cut into four quarters.
7   To re-heat, place on a tray in a pre-heated oven at 185°C/gas mark 4 for 15-20 minutes or until piping hot and crackly.
8   Serve with potatoes and vegetables of your choice. A grain mustard mash and purple sprouting broccoli work well.

Top Tip: If the crackling doesn't crackle, finish under the grill for a few moments. It will puff up before your eyes.

James Chapman, Executive Head Chef, Victoria Inn, Salcombe

"We have used this recipe in many different guises over the years; it's a constant favourite and has never waned in popularity. Make sure you use good-quality pork that's not wet and is scored well. The oil works as a rendering agent on the fat, so even though it's cooked in oil it's not a greasy dish.

Preparation is my top tip, and I would also say don't be afraid to experiment. If you don't have a certain ingredient, try something else. It may become your new favourite; this is how some of the best recipes have evolved.

The drive, dedication and commitment of our proprietors, Tim and Liz Hore, at the Victoria Inn, mean I head up one of the best, most talented and supportive team of chefs I have ever worked with."

Rachel Bell, Marketing Director, Bell & Loxton, South Milton

"As a busy working mum I am always looking at healthy ways to feed the family, so I like to source food using our local butcher and farmers' markets where possible. Our award-winning rapeseed oil is grown, pressed and bottled on the family farm.

My husband, Jonathan, and I, along with his parents, started the business five years ago, after looking at ways to make the family farm more sustainable. Jonathan's passion for traceability in food helped lead to the birth of Bell & Loxton. The highlight of our company's achievements so far was achieving three stars and being named one of the top 50 national products at the Great Taste Awards in 2013. To be recognised nationally is a massive achievement.

Our oil is very versatile and can be used for dressings, dipping, stir-fries and roasting – it makes fantastic roast potatoes! We are stocked in farm shops and delicatessens throughout Devon, regional Waitrose stores and online."

Outdoor-reared local pork belly cooked in Hunter's Crispy Pig beer

Recipe by Nick Cottrell, Head Chef, Dolphin House Brazzerie, Sutton Harbour, Plymouth

Ingredients

1kg boned belly pork (ask your butcher to remove the skin and keep it)
2 cooking apples
4 small eating apples
1 onion
2 sticks of celery
1 small piece of root ginger
1 bottle of Hunter's Crispy Pig beer
Cornish sea salt and freshly ground black pepper to season

Method

1 Prepare the vegetables by coarsely chopping the onion, celery, ginger and two cooking apples. Place in a roasting tin, sit the pork on top and cover with the beer. Wrap in cling film and refrigerate for 8 hours or overnight.

2 Remove the dish from fridge and take off the cling film. Season with salt and pepper and cover with baking parchment and two layers of foil, if you're not using a lid. Place in pre-heated oven 140°C/gas mark 1 for 5 hours.

3 About 30 minutes before the pork is cooked, put the 4 eating apples, scored around the middle and wrapped in foil, into the oven. Remove them at the same time as the pork and keep wrapped up until needed.

4 Meanwhile, to cook the crackling, cut the skin into thin strips, salt and put in the oven, pre-heated to the maximum temperature, for 20 minutes.

5 Remove the pork from the roasting tin and let it rest while you strain the vegetable juices into a pan (discard the vegetables). Bring to a rolling boil and reduce the liquid by half, to a syrupy consistency.

6 Cut the pork into four, place it fat side down on a griddle pan for 15 seconds, then place each piece on a warmed plate, dress with the juices and serve with crackling and a baked apple. (This dish tastes great with a smooth mash and greens with walnut butter.)

Nick Cottrell, Head Chef, Dolphin House Brazzerie, Sutton Harbour, Plymouth

"The inspiration for this recipe is simple: the beer. Our local, outdoor-reared Poltimore Farm pork dish is also extremely popular with our customers. It was fantastic coming across Hunter's Brewery and its speciality Crispy Pig beer, which uses fresh apples and is bottle conditioned – perfect for my dish. I am often asked how to get good crackling with pork: I think I have this covered in my recipe!

Working at Dolphin House is a great and exciting opportunity, particularly as it means working with family and collaborating with a fantastic team who believe in the importance of good food with great provenance. Last year (2014) saw much recognition for what we do and made us all proud of what we have achieved. Being a chef involves long hours and hard work, so you have to love it. We all agree it is that passion which drives us."

Paul Walker, owner, Hunter's Brewery, Ipplepen

"We make real ale in cask and bottles and are proud to be the only brewery in Devon with an automated bottling plant that produces bottle-conditioned beer. We are passionate about our bottled ale remaining unpasteurised and unfiltered, so it still contains live yeast that continues to ferment in the bottle, adding more flavour.

We supply many pubs in South Devon and our bottles are also available through wholesalers across Devon and into Somerset.

For us, quality is the top factor. When sourcing ingredients for beer, it is important to look for malt with a good yield and alpha content.

Our proudest moment recently was seeing the first batches of beer labelled with our new branding coming off the automated bottling line: it was a long journey for us to get the process up and running."

Barbecued spatchcock chicken with Waterhouse Fayre Lime Pickle, mango pickled ginger, naan bread croutons and mango chutney dressing

Recipe by Simon Tucker, Head Chef, The Royal Oak Inn, Meavy, Dartmoor

Ingredients
1 spatchcock chicken
1 jar of Waterhouse Fayre Lime Pickle

For the salad
1 ripe mango
25g pickled ginger
200g fresh mixed salad leaves
Half a cucumber, deseeded and skinned
12 cherry tomatoes, halved
Two large garlic naan breads
Olive oil

For the dressing
2 tbsp mango chutney
5 tbsp mayonnaise
10 tbsp olive oil

To prepare and cook the chicken
1 Spread the lime pickle over the chicken and marinate for up to 48 hours.
2 Cook in a preheated oven at 180°C/gas mark 4 for about 40 minutes, until the juices run clear.

To make the salad
1 Cut around the stone of the mango, remove it, scoop out the flesh and roughly dice to make different-sized mango pieces.
2 Shred the pickled ginger very thinly, then add the sliced cucumber, salad leaves and halved tomatoes and mix together with the mango.
3 Cut the naan bread into squares, put into a bowl and evenly coat in a little olive oil.
4 Place the squares of bread on a baking tray and toast in a medium oven until golden brown. Just before serving, scatter them evenly over the top of the salad.

To make the dressing
Blitz all the ingredients with a hand blender.

Continued on page 117…

To barbecue and serve
Sear the cooked chicken on the barbecue for about 10 minutes on each side, then serve with the salad and dressing.

"When making preserves, jams or chutneys, always use the best-quality produce, which should be ripe or slightly under-ripe."

Ann Stallard

Ann Stallard, Waterhouse Fayre, Burlescombe

"My husband, Neil, and I started growing some different varieties of raspberries, along with other berries not so commonly available, mainly for the catering trade. While Neil is the fruit growing expert, I had to learn how to make jams and chutneys to use the surplus. This resulted in me having a market stall on a Saturday in South Molton to sell the preserves. That was eleven years ago, and we now use all the fruit we grow in our Waterhouse Fayre preserves.

I love coming up with new recipes. Lime Pickle is my newest creation, but I must thank my tasting panel for their input: my niece Sophie and her colleagues in Worcester, who originate from Pakistan."

Simon Tucker, Head Chef, The Royal Oak Inn, Meavy, Dartmoor

"I chose this recipe because I wanted to create something easy to prepare that could be enjoyed by all on a nice summer's day. A local butcher can spatchcock the chicken for you. Make sure you part cook it (until about 90% done) in the oven, before putting on the barbecue, as you are only finishing it on the barbecue to give it a flame-grilled taste.

A top cooking tip is do not be afraid to experiment. If you enjoy two ingredients then there is no reason why they wouldn't work together. If you are unsure about trying it for yourself, search the internet – there is bound to be someone who has already tried your idea!"

Homemade Scotch egg, using sausage from Pork Heaven from Devon

Recipe by Robert Smallbone, Head Chef, The Grove Inn, King's Nympton

Ingredients
4 whole eggs
3 beaten eggs
6 rashers of smoked dry-cured streaky bacon
380g sausage meat from Pork Heaven from Devon
Panko (Japanese) breadcrumbs

Top Tip: Avoid blitzing the crispy bacon too much. It's nice to have chunky pieces of crisp bacon mixed in with the soft sausage meat as a contrast in texture.

Method
1 Preheat the oven to 240°C/gas mark 9.
2 Bring a pan of water to the boil.
3 Place the bacon rashers on a cooling rack over a roasting tray and put them in the oven for five minutes. Turn down the temperature to 190°C/gas mark 5 and cook for a further 20 minutes, turning the rashers over a couple of times during cooking. In the end you will have totally crispy bacon.
4 Gently place the eggs into the boiling water and boil for exactly 6½ minutes, then plunge into cold water to stop them cooking further. Peel carefully.
5 Blitz the cooled crispy bacon in a food processor, remove, then set aside.
6 In the same processor add the sausage meat, then blend with the cooked bacon. Place in the fridge to chill.
7 Heat a deep-fat fryer or pan of oil.
8 Weigh out 95g of sausage meat, mould into a flat disk and form around the egg until fully coated. Repeat the process with the other three eggs.
9 Coat the Scotch eggs in the beaten egg, then the breadcrumbs.
10 Gently place in the hot oil and cook for five minutes.
11 Leave to rest on kitchen roll, then serve with homemade mayonnaise and salad leaves.

Robert Smallbone, Head Chef, The Grove Inn, King's Nympton

"I've always loved a well-made Scotch egg and I create different recipes for them at the Grove Inn, as well as for my own personal enjoyment. I wanted this recipe to be a simple celebration of the pig!

My favourite ingredient is garlic: it works with meat, fish poultry and vegetables. My advice to budding chefs is if you can read, you can follow *any* recipe!

The best part of my job is meeting people and hearing their stories. Another highlight was when I was asked to submit my 'Laver bread & scallop soup' recipe to Carol Trewin for her *Devon Cook Book*. It was, sadly, her last book; a great loss.

I unwind by seeking out great company, great music, great food and great wine!"

Jeannie Morrissey and Willy Knowles, Pork Heaven from Devon, Stoodliegh Barton, near Tiverton

"We breed, rear and farm pigs, and grow corn for their feed and bedding. Predominantly outdoor-reared, there are 60 pigs, including seven breeding sows and one boar. We're proud to say we go from seed to feed and pork to fork all on the farm, apart from the weekly abattoir visit.

What I love about pig farming is being my own boss. One of my most dangerous moments in the job was when our tractor, Old Clonkie, took off down a steep field with me in it. We now have a newer beast, Matilda Massey, who comes complete with brakes, a working clutch, lights and even a radio!

We both agree that winning the Champion Product at the Taste of the West Awards for our Butcher's Classic Pork Sausages was our proudest moment. We were both so shocked, Willy was speechless, which is most rare!

My advice to anyone is when sourcing ingredients always go for the very best."

Roasted, marinated loin of venison from M C Kelly, with pears, juniper and red cabbage

Recipe by Scott Paton, Head Chef, The Horn of Plenty, Gulworthy, Tavistock

For the marinated venison
700g boned-out loin of venison, cut
   into four 175g portions
1 bottle of red wine
175ml glass sloe gin
2 shallots, finely chopped
15 juniper berries, crushed
1 clove of garlic, chopped
50ml olive oil
50g butter
225g bramble jelly
300ml game stock
Salt and pepper

For the red cabbage
1 shallot, finely chopped
50g butter
Half a small red cabbage, finely
   shredded
2 Cox apples, peeled and chopped
Pinch of nutmeg
175ml glass red wine vinegar
3 cloves
50g bramble jelly
100g sugar

For the pears
2 Conference pears peeled and
   cored

1l stock syrup (1l water, 1kg sugar)
8 crushed juniper berries
One shot of Plymouth Gin

To marinate the venison
1   Mix the red wine, sloe gin, shallots, juniper berries, garlic and olive oil in a bowl and marinate the venison in it for 24 hours.
2   When you are ready to cook the dish, remove the venison from the marinade. Strain the liquid into a jug and set aside.
3   Sweat the shallots, juniper berries and garlic from the marinade in the butter, then add the bramble jelly, game stock and strained liquid from the marinade.
4   Reduce the mixture quickly by heating rapidly, until slightly thickened. Season and set aside.

To cook the red cabbage
1   Cook the shallot over a medium heat in the butter, then add the red cabbage.
2   Sweat for 5 minutes, then add the apple, nutmeg, vinegar, cloves, bramble jelly and sugar, and simmer gently for a further 35 minutes. Set aside and keep warm.

To cook the venison
1   Seal the venison fillets in a hot pan with a little oil.
2   Season, then place in the oven at 200°C/gas mark 6 for

Continued on page 125...

5 minutes (if the fillets are thin, 3-4 minutes will do).

3 Remove from the oven and rest in a warm place for 7-8 minutes.

To cook the pears

1 Bring the stock syrup to the boil to infuse the juniper and gin, then remove from the heat.

2 Drop the pears in and leave to cool. (You might need to use a small plate to stop the pears from floating above the syrup level.) If the pears are very ripe, remove them earlier from the liquid to stop them going too soft.

To serve

Slice the pears into wedges of eight, using four slices per portion, then place a spoonful of red cabbage next to them. Carve the venison portions into five pieces and place on top of the cabbage. Finish by drizzling some of the reduced marinade around the plate.

Scott Paton, Head Chef, The Horn of Plenty, Gulworthy, Tavistock, Devon

"This recipe is a classic in our repertoire at The Horn of Plenty. The inspiration came from the beautiful venison saddles that are available from the Hatherleigh estate. My top tip for this dish is to avoid over-cooking the venison; it's definitely at its tastiest when nice and pink.

We have spectacular produce coming through the door every day here, so it's hard to pinpoint just one favourite ingredient. They change throughout the seasons.

If I had to give a top tip to budding chefs/cooks it would be to master the basics, find a great mentor and stick with it!

When I'm not working I like to spend time with my young family. They really help me with creativity and somehow make it all worthwhile."

Andy Gray, Managing Director, M C Kelly, Copplestone, Crediton

"As a poultry and arable farmer, a catering butcher, processor of wild shot game and venison, as well as wholesalers of fine foods, M C Kelly supplies a wide range of catering customers and butchers.

I believe that reliability of supply is crucial when sourcing ingredients. If you don't have it in your kitchen when you need to cook it, you're in trouble!

Our company lives by the mantra 'Provenance, Quality and Service', believing that if a product delivers on these three fronts, it's usually a winner.

The best and worst parts of my job are my colleagues and my colleagues! Seriously, though, I am continually proud of what the team achieves. I find creating and maintaining good relationships with our customers a vital part of the job.

Out of work, I enjoy fishing, falconry and deer stalking."

Vanilla cheesecake with an almond tuille and Orange Elephant Pink Grapefruit Sorbet

Recipe by Scott Paton, The Horn of Plenty

For the cheesecake

2 packets of digestive biscuits
125g butter
750g mascarpone
125g icing sugar
350ml milk
350g double cream, whipped
3 vanilla pods
9 pre-soaked gelatine leaves

For the tuille

50g soft butter
50g glucose
50g ground almonds
Zest of an orange

To finish

Two generous scoops of Orange
   Elephant Pink Grapefruit Sorbet
2 pink grapefruit

To make the cheesecake

1 In a food processor blitz the biscuits until they become a fine crumb. Melt the butter and fold together.
2 Place the biscuit mixture into a cling-filmed tray, evenly spread it by pressing down with the back of a spoon.
3 Place the milk and vanilla pods in a pan and bring to the boil. Remove from the heat, strain the milk to remove the vanilla pods, then add the pre-soaked gelatine leaves.
4 Place the mascarpone and icing sugar in a bowl and mix until smooth. Add the milk, stir until smooth, then fold in the whipped cream until completely mixed.
5 Pour onto the biscuit base and allow to set in the fridge for at least three hours.

To make the tuille

1 Mix all the ingredients in an electric mixer and allow to rest in the fridge for one hour.
2 Once chilled, roll it into a thin sausage shape about 8cm long. Place on a baking sheet and cook at 180°C/gas mark 4 for 10 minutes. When cooked, trim the tuille to the same size as the cheesecake and place it on top.

To serve

1 Cut the cheesecake into 8cm x 4cm portions using a hot knife.
2 Segment the grapefruit and place on top of the cheesecake portions.
3 Serve with a generous scoop of Orange Elephant Pink Grapefruit Sorbet.

"I describe myself as owner, manager, ice cream maker, calf-rearer, as well as mum, at the Orange Elephant Ice Cream Parlour on our Devon farm."

Helen Taverner,
Taverner's Farm, Kennford

Seared Lyme Bay scallops with Burrow Farm Black Pudding, celeriac and apple purée and a cider reduction

Recipe by Franck Favereaux, Head Chef, Otterton Mill, Otterton

Ingredients

12 Lyme Bay scallops (without roe)
2 whole Burrow Farm black puddings, cut into 12 x 1cm slices
1 tbsp olive oil
400g celeriac, peeled and cut into 3cm cubes
2 eating apples, peeled, cored and cut into small cubes
800ml milk
2 bay leaves
Pinch of salt
Pepper
500ml local cider
500ml beef stock
50g butter
Micro-herbs to garnish

Method

1 Put the celeriac, milk, bay leaves and salt into a pan and bring to the boil. Simmer for 10 minutes, then add the diced apples and simmer for a further 10 minutes. Drain and remove the bay leaves, but keep the milk.

2 Puree this mixture in a food processor until smooth, using some of the milk. Keep it warm.

3 Reduce the cider in another pan until it reaches a syrupy consistency. Add the stock and reduce further. Add the diced butter and whisk into the sauce. Season as required, then pass through a fine sieve. Set aside.

4 Heat a non-stick frying pan and add the olive oil. Fry the black pudding slices on both sides until crispy (about 1-2 minutes on each side). Drain on kitchen paper.

5 Season the scallops.

6 In the same pan, add a little oil and sear the scallops over a high heat for 1-2 minutes on both sides until caramelised (this can be done in batches).

7 To serve, place the celeriac and apple purée in the centre of a warm plate, and arrange three slices of black pudding, alternating with three scallops, around the puree. Drizzle with the cider reduction, and garnish with some micro-herbs.

Top Tip: When searing the scallops, make sure you use a very hot pan.

> "Keep things simple, and buy the best cared-for produce you can find locally."
>
> Franck Favereaux

Franck Favereaux, Head Chef, Otterton Mill, Otterton

"I have been Head Chef at Otterton Mill since February 2012, and used to be the proprietor of The Seafood Restaurant in Exmouth, which I ran for ten years with my wife, Sarah. A French native, I have worked and lived in the UK since 1989, previously working throughout the South of France in Michelin starred restaurants. Since joining the Mill, I have brought a French twist to the Mill's style of rustic British food."

Neil and Sally Grigg, Burrow Farm, Broadclyst

"We started tenant farming at Burrow Farm eight years ago, when we established our herd of pedigree Red Ruby Devon cattle. As direct sales of our own produce grew, we bought the long-established Courtneys Butchers of Cowick Steet in Exeter in 2013. It has since been renamed Burrow Farm @ Courtneys.

As well as selling beef in the shop, we have kept the traditional recipes and products that have been made there for four generations. These include Courtney's sausages, hogs' pudding and an award-winning black pudding. Mike Lavis and his wife, Carol (née Courtney), have passed on these age-old recipes, and Mike continues to work in the shop making black puddings to the same recipe, just as he has done for the past 40 years."

Smoked cheese and toasted seed croquettes with Hillside's Pear, Apple & Herb Chutney

Recipe by Jay Allan, Hillside Foods, Exeter

For the croquettes
1kg potatoes (for mash)
30g butter
5g sea salt
1g cracked pepper
1 tbsp chopped flat-leaf parsley
250g Quickes smoked cheese
1l sunflower oil

For the crumb
1 packet of Hillside Oat & Seed
    biscuits (130g)
30g pumpkin seeds, chopped
10g poppy seeds
10g sesame seeds
30g chopped hazelnuts
3g fennel seeds
3g cumin seeds
4g sea salt
1g cracked pepper
Eggs (for egg wash)
Plain flour (for dusting)

For serving
1 jar of Hillside Pear, Apple & Herb
    Chutney
Celery leaves
Red apple
Chicory

To make the mash
1 Wash, peel and chop the potatoes into even-sized pieces and rinse thoroughly. Place in a pan of cold salted water and bring to the boil, then simmer for 10 minutes or until the potatoes are just cooked. Do not overcook or the potatoes will become wet.
2 Drain well in a colander for 20 minutes and cool.
3 Press the potato through a fine sieve, ensuring that there are no lumps, then season with salt and pepper, melted butter and chopped parsley.
4 Mix well until smooth and well bound.

To make the crumb
1 In a food processor, lightly blitz the biscuits until they form a light crumb.
2 Add all the seeds, nuts and seasoning to the mix.

To make the croquettes
1 Cut the cheese into 6 x 2cm rectangles.
2 Lightly dust the cheese in flour, then mould the mashed potato around the cheese, trying to make them into cylinders.
3 Place them in the fridge to firm up for 30 minutes.
4 Once cold, roll the croquettes in the flour, dust off the excess, then coat in the egg wash, then the crumb mix. Repeat a couple of times until there is an even layer of crumb coating.
5 Re-shape the croquettes, then return to the fridge to cool and set firmly.

Continued on page 135...

6 Heat the oil to 180°C and place the croquettes into it. Once golden brown, remove from the oil, drain on some kitchen roll, and sprinkle with fine sea salt to season.

7 Serve with the chutney and a light salad of celery leaves, chicory and red apple.

Jay Allan, Hillside Foods, Exeter

"Hillside Foods was founded in 2008. Since then we have been dedicated to creating the ultimate cheeseboard accompaniments. Our award-winning range comprises savoury biscuits, fruit cheeses, pickles and chutneys, and our kitchen is a place where creativity, tradition and the finest ingredients come together to create our recipes.

When creating products for the cheeseboard, we have always looked to local artisan cheese producers and sourced seasonal fruit and vegetables. As we develop new lines we consider colour, texture, shape, but above all the flavours and flavour combinations in our biscuits, fruit cheeses, pickles and chutneys.

When sourcing ingredients, our ethos is to follow the seasons closely to get produce at its best.

The most challenging part of my job is working with family! But on a serious note, I am very proud that we are a flourishing business and continue to win lots of awards."

Cornwall

Ham hock and Kittow's Butchers' Cornish Hogs Pudding terrine

Recipe by Ken Symons, Head Chef, Oliver's, Falmouth

Ingredients

2 ham hocks (approx 800g)

Bouquet garni

250g (1 stick) Kittow's Cornish Hogs Pudding, cut into pea-sized cubes

4 spring onions, finely chopped

2 tbsp snipped chives

2 tbsp chopped parsley

1 tbsp grain mustard

10ml apple juice

50ml cooking liquor

1 large Bramley apple, peeled and roughly chopped

Sprig of thyme

25g caster sugar

Salt and pepper

Method

1   Put the ham hocks in a large saucepan, cover with water and add the bouquet garni. Bring to the boil and simmer for approximately four hours, or until the meat starts to leave the bone.

2   Once cooked, gently remove the ham from the liquor and leave it to cool for 20 minutes. Strain 50ml of the liquor and reserve it. Remove the meat's skin and place the meat in a large mixing bowl.

3   In a small saucepan, place the apple, sugar and sprig of thyme, gently heat and cook for 10 minutes to make an apple sauce. Put to one side.

4   Put the hogs pudding in a non-stick pan and dry-fry for a couple of minutes, or until crisp and golden.

5   Add the herbs, half of the apple sauce, fried hogs pudding, mustard, apple juice and reserved liquor to the ham meat. Gently fold the mixture and season to taste.

6   Place the mixture on cling-film, make a large sausage shape and wrap tightly. Refrigerate to set for about four hours.

7   To serve, spread a little of the reserved apple sauce onto four plates, top with a little tossed salad, diced apple and fresh mint leaves. Remove the terrine from the fridge and unwrap. Slice into 8 equal pieces, placing two on each plate. Enjoy with a good-quality, crisp bread.

James Kittow,
Kittow's Butchers, Par

"Kittow's Butchers has been run by my family for five generations. We have our own pedigree herd of Red Ruby cattle and we work closely with a small number of farmers who produce pork, lamb and beef for us. If I were to give customers one top tip, it would be to choose meat that shows quality over price.

I'm always busy and love my job, working with great team members and staff. I'm also active in the community and with schools, providing demonstrations to help people understand the food industry and opportunities within it. We are soon opening a bespoke farm shop on site too.

As for my free time, I am the youngest member of the Lostwithiel Rotary Club, where we meet once a week and enjoy a beer. I also like to walk the dogs around the farm in the evening, perhaps with a couple of cans of beer too!"

Lynher Dairies' Cornish Yarg, shallot and saffron tart

Recipe by Ken Symons, Head Chef, Oliver's, Falmouth

For the pastry

200g plain flour
150g unsalted butter, diced
Pinch of Cornish sea salt
1 egg
25ml whipping cream
50g Cornish yarg, finely grated
Generous pinch of grated nutmeg

For the filling

3 medium banana shallots, finely
    chopped
Good pinch of saffron
Butter for frying
100ml cider vinegar
300g Cornish yarg, cut into 2cm
    cubes (Do not remove the nettle)
3 eggs, beaten
250ml double cream
Cornish sea salt and freshly ground
    pepper
1 tbsp snipped chives

To make the pastry

1 Place the flour, butter, salt and nutmeg in a food
   processor and pulse together to form fine crumbs.
2 Add the remaining ingredients and pulse to form a ball of
   dough. Remove, wrap in cling-film and place in the fridge
   for an hour to set.
3 Grease and line a 25cm flan ring and place on a flat
   baking tray. Roll out the pastry to 3-4mm thick and line
   the case. Cover the base with baking paper and ceramic
   beads and bake blind in a preheated oven at 180°C/gas
   mark 4 for 15–18 minutes, until crisp and golden.
4 Remove the paper and beads.

To make the filling

1 Place a small skillet over a gentle heat, add a little butter
   and cook the shallots and saffron until soft.
2 Add the vinegar, turn up the heat and reduce until almost
   dry. Remove from the heat.
3 Spread this mixture evenly over the base of the tart,
   sprinkle with the chives and cover with the cubed
   cheese.
4 Whisk together the eggs and cream, season with salt and
   pepper, and pour into the tart.
5 Bake at 180°C/gas mark 4 for 25-30 minutes, or until
   golden with a little wobble. Remove and leave to set for
   20 minutes.

To serve

This tart is excellent for lunch with a simple salad. We serve
it with a little wild asparagus and a 'feta' salad made with
yarg.

"... our foragers pick four tonnes of nettle and wild garlic leaves from the Ponsanooth woodlands each spring."

Catherine Mead

Ken Symons, Head Chef, Oliver's, Falmouth

"I am a very lucky chef, being surrounded by such fantastic produce. I love being able to constantly change the menu, phoning my local suppliers for fish, foraged goods and fresh perishables. My passion for great, fresh Cornish produce never wavers. I simply love food – cooking, eating and growing it. I have a great life in a fabulous part of the country.

I relax with my chef friends when we meet up once a month through the Cornish Chefs' Club. We cook for each other at our own establishments, and talk food – it's a chef thing.

One of my career highlights was having the pleasure of working alongside Gordon Ramsay and the late Charlie Trotter at the Dorchester Hotel in London. It was a really humbling experience."

Catherine Mead, Lynher Dairies Cheese Company, Ponsanooth, Truro

"The question we are most frequently asked about Cornish Yarg is: how did it get its name? The answer: from the reverse spelling of its creator's surname, Alan Gray.

The next question is often about whether the nettle leaves still sting. The answer is no, which is just as well, given that our foragers pick four tonnes of nettle and wild garlic leaves from the Ponsanooth woodlands each spring.

Handmade in open vats, the semi-hard cheese takes on the flavour of the leaves in which it is wrapped. Nettles impart a mushroomy taste, with the wild garlic whispering rather than shouting its name.

I am also an international cheese judge and authority on artisan British cheese. In fact, we're all cheese judges at Lynher, regularly sampling our Yargs for taste, texture, appearance and acidity. Consistence and excellence, that's what we aim for."

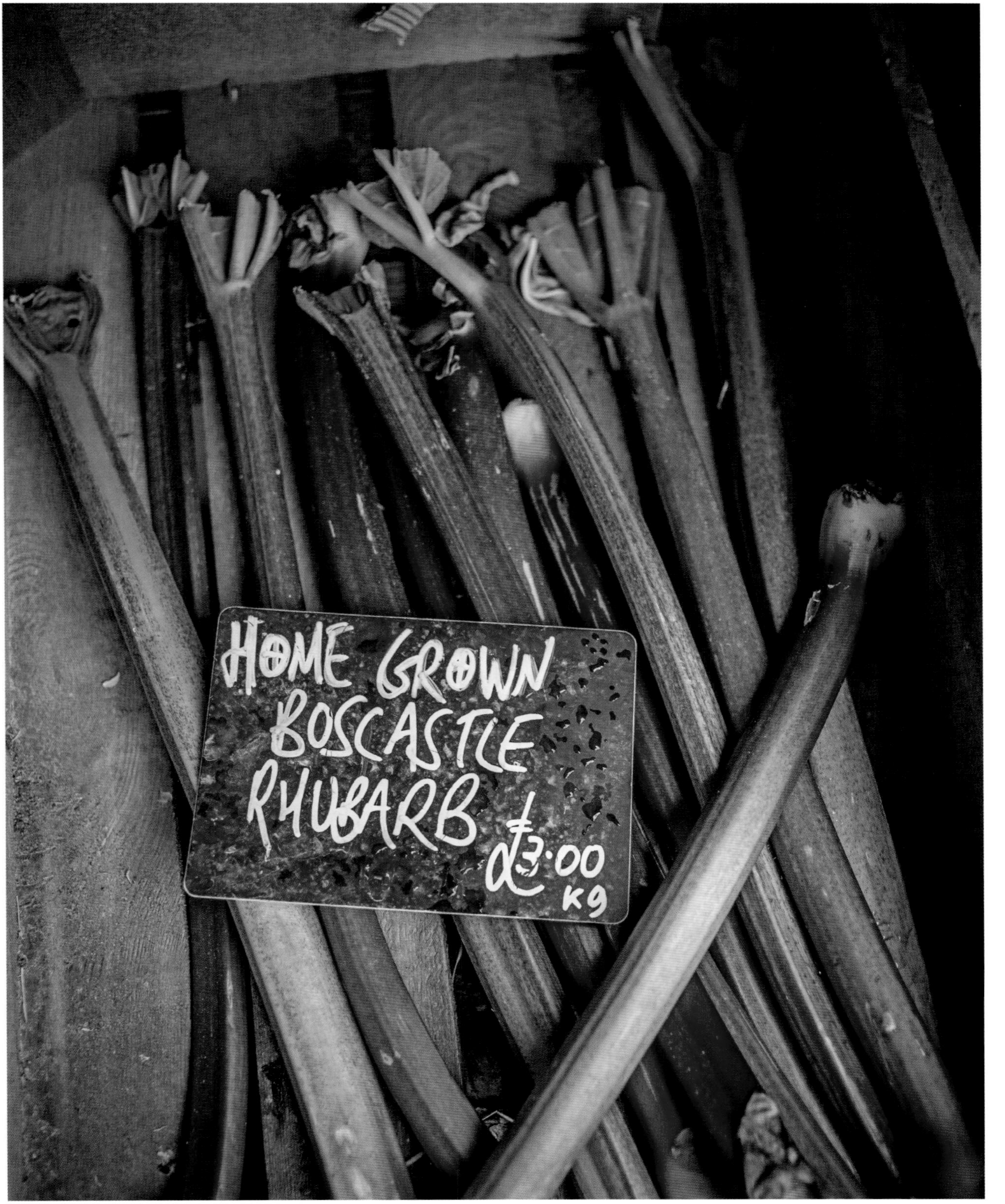
HOME GROWN
BOSCASTLE
RHUBARB
£3·00
kg

Crispy Cornish scallops with Artisan Malt Vinegar

Recipe by Tom Mackins, Head Chef, Falmouth Bay Seafood Café, Truro

For the scallops

12 large Cornish scallops (cleaned)
1 egg
60g Panko breadcrumbs
Oil for frying

For the vinegar dip

400ml Artisan Malt Vinegar
¼ tbsp ground bay leaves
¼ tbsp celery salt
¼ tbsp dry mustard
¼ tsp ground black pepper
¼ tsp ground ginger
¼ tsp sweet paprika
¼ tsp ground white pepper
¼ tsp ground nutmeg
¼ tsp ground cloves
¼ tsp ground allspice

Method

1 Beat the egg in a small mixing bowl.
2 One at a time, dip the scallops into the egg, then into the breadcrumbs and set aside until needed.
3 In another mixing bowl, place all the spices and herbs and mix well, adding the vinegar last.
4 Heat the oil in a frying pan and add the scallops one by one. Cook for about one minute until golden on one side, then turn over and cook for 30 seconds or so on the second side.
5 Once both sides are golden, take the scallops out of the pan and serve with the vinegar dip.

Top Tip: Remember that scallops can overcook very easily, so work quickly and ensure that all ingredients are to hand.

Tom Mackins, Head Chef, Falmouth Bay Seafood Café, Truro

"My inspiration for this recipe? As I clearly love working with seafood, I decided to use something that at first glance wouldn't appear to go with vinegar.

I like the challenge of using a new ingredient, something I haven't used before, as I can then experiment with it. It's important to have confidence in the kitchen – lots of it!

Over the last 11 years, I've had many kitchen dramas. I think trying to complete a service with no extraction and the kitchen temperature being well over 80 degrees was among my most challenging evenings.

I feel so lucky to be able to do what I can do and what I love to do, all day. It doesn't even feel like a job the majority of the time."

Mark and Leonora Nattrass, Partners, The Artisan Malt Vinegar Company, Coverack

"Our company is based in a former nuclear bunker in the depths of the countryside, which was an early-warning station from the Cold War days. We use this vast, cold space to brew and oak-mature the vinegar in small batches by traditional methods. The result is something mellow and flavourful, an age away from the usual malt vinegar you sprinkle on your chips. It is the only gourmet malt vinegar currently available in the UK.

We supply delicatessens and restaurants across the country. The vinegar's success has been underpinned by ten years' experience of brewing fine real ales in our microbrewery, Lizard Ales, which is run from the same premises. We also have a smallholding on site, with poultry, vegetables and sometimes pigs, and Mark is a keen boat fisherman. We are always busy!"

Cornish mackerel, baby beets, watercress and crispy shallots with Trewithen Dairy yoghurt

Recipe by Adam Vasey, Head Chef, No.4 Peterville, St Agnes

Ingredients

2 large mackerel, gutted and filleted
 (Ask your fishmonger to do this if
 you don't feel confident.)
4 tbsp Trewithen Dairy natural yoghurt
6 raw baby beetroot
100g watercress
2 banana shallots
100ml red wine vinegar
100ml red wine
70g castor sugar
1 egg, beaten
1 tbsp plain flour
2 tbsp Panko breadcrumbs
Vegetable oil for frying
Sea salt

To cook the crispy shallots

1 Peel the banana shallots and cut into fine rings.
2 Put the red wine vinegar, red wine and sugar into a saucepan. Bring to the boil until the sugar dissolves, then add the shallot rings. Take the mixture off the heat and leave for 2-3 hours to infuse.
3 Once the shallots have taken on a nice red colour, drain them and coat each ring in flour, then egg, then breadcrumbs.
4 Just before serving, fry the shallot rings in vegetable oil until golden. Set them on kitchen roll to soak up any excess oil and sprinkle a good pinch of sea salt over the top.

To prepare the beetroot and watercress

1 Boil the beets for about 8–10 minutes until a knife can pass through them easily.
2 Drain the water, peel the beetroot and cut them into halves.
3 Pick the watercress into individual leaves to dress the dish.

To cook the mackerel

1 Get a sauté or frying pan really nice and hot on the stove.
2 Cut each mackerel in half, so that each fish provides two portions.
3 Oil the pan, then put the mackerel fillets in skin side down until the skin turns crispy and golden. Take the pan off the heat and turn the fish over to flesh side down. Leave to cook through for 1 minute.

Continued on page 155...

To serve

1 Spread a tablespoon of Trewithen Dairy natural yoghurt in a swirl on each plate.
2 Add 3 halves of baby beets to each plate and dress with a few leaves of watercress.
3 Place the mackerel on the plates and sprinkle with the crispy shallot rings. Serve straight away.

"In the early days, with our own herds, we would bottle the milk once the children were in bed and deliver it early next morning before they woke."

Bill and Rachel Clarke, Trewithen Dairy, Greymare Farm, near Lostwithiel

"Our families have been dairy farmers for generations and our own experience goes back more than 25 years. It has taken all our expertise – and plenty of patience – to build the business to its current position.

In the early days, with our own herds, we would bottle the milk once the children were in bed and deliver it early next morning before they woke. We made the clotted cream ourselves and potted it by hand. Then, encouraged by a local shopkeeper, we began selling our products under the Trewithen Dairy label. Soon after we started this, in 1994, restaurants, hotels, garages and more shops joined the ranks of satisfied customers.

Recent years have seen sons Francis and George join the business, which now has more than 130 employees and is Cornwall and Devon's largest milk bottler.

Our products include an award-winning range of milk, butter and cream of various types, plus of course the Taste of the West Gold award Natural Yoghurt as well as new Toffee & Apple and Strawberry & Honey yoghurts."

Whole grilled plaice, with mussel and saffron butter and croquettes using Primrose Herd's chorizo

Recipe by Adam Vasey, Head Chef, No.4 Peterville, St Agnes

Ingredients
4 whole plaice

For the croquettes
1 large potato
2-3 Primrose Herd chorizo sausages
300ml milk
75g plain flour
50g unsalted butter
35g freshly grated parmesan
1 egg, beaten
4 tbsp Panko breadcrumbs

For the butter
1.5kg mussels
70g unsalted butter
2 pinches of saffron
1 large potato
100ml white wine
2 chorizo sausages, crumbled
Squeeze of lemon juice

Pea shoots for garnish

Top Tip: Make the croquettes in advance and refrigerate until you need them. Warm them in the oven just before you serve the dish.

To make the croquettes
1 Chop up and boil the potato until cooked.
2 Open up the sausages and pan-fry the meat in a splash of vegetable oil for 2-3 minutes.
3 Blitz the potato and meat together in a food processor.
4 Now make a béchamel sauce. Melt the butter in a saucepan, keep the pan on the heat and add the flour. Stir for about three minutes until the flour has cooked out. Add the milk a little at a time and keep stirring until the mixture thickens and has a smooth consistency with no lumps. Add the parmesan and stir.
5 Combine the béchamel sauce with the sausage and potato mix in a food processor.
6 Shape the mixture into a log, about 2.5cm wide, on a floured surface and cut into inch-long croquettes.
7 Dip the croquettes into a little flour, then egg, then breadcrumbs.
8 Just before serving, deep-fry the croquettes in vegetable oil for a couple of minutes at 165°C, until golden.

To make the butter
1 Chop a potato into half inch cubes, place in a pan and cover with water. Add a pinch of salt and 2 pinches of saffron. Bring to the boil and cook for about five minutes until the potato is cooked but not falling apart. Drain and leave.
2 Cook the mussels in a good slug of white wine for 5 minutes until their shells open. De-shell them, removing any beards.

Continued on page 159...

3 Roughly crumble the chorizo sausage meat, pan-fry it in vegetable oil until cooked through for about 2-3 minutes.
4 Melt the butter in a pan with a squeeze of lemon juice. Add the mussels, potato cubes and cooked chorizo to the butter.

To cook the fish
1 Set the grill to high and oil a tray.
2 Place the fish on the tray and cook under the grill for 7-8 minutes until it feels firm and cooked through.

To serve
Place the fish on warmed plates, add the butter, then garnish with the croquettes and some pea shoots.

Adam Vasey, No.4 Peterville, St Agnes

"We like to pair the land with the sea in a lot of the dishes in the restaurant, so we work to try to incorporate these two elements together.

This recipe takes a bit of preparation but it's worth it – the chorizo croquettes are light and go fabulously with the fish.

This dish can be made with any flat fish really; we've done it with plaice as it was plentiful at the time, but you can use lemon sole, megrim sole or even bass when in season.

My favourite ingredient is butter – certainly not great for your waistline, but it makes everything taste amazing! And bones – we use bone marrow to serve with our steaks, and veal bones and chicken carcasses to make vats of stock."

Bill and Sally Lugg, Primrose Herd, Redruth

"We farm traditional breed pigs, specialising in pedigree Gloucestershire Old Spots, Large Blacks and British Saddlebacks. The pork is supplied to retail and wholesale customers throughout the UK.

We process our products in the farm's butchery, including dry-cured bacon, Cornish hogs' pudding, gammon and cooked ham, plus a range of fresh pork, smoked products and charcuterie.

The worst part of our job must be having to say goodbye to a breeding pig that is almost part of the family. On the plus side, we still get a thrill when someone says they have enjoyed our pork cooked to perfection by one of Cornwall's leading chefs."

Smoked posh Scotch egg with a kedgeree salad

Recipe by Matthew Rowe, Head Chef and Landlord, The Falmouth Packet Inn, Rosudgeon, near Penzance

For the Scotch eggs

4 Cornish duck eggs cracked into separate cups
3 tbsp white wine vinegar
400g smoked salmon
200g breadcrumbs
2 eggs for egg wash
150g flour or ground rice

For the kedgeree salad

140g mixed salad leaves
4 hot-smoked mackerel fillets from Wing of St Mawes
300g cooked saffron rice and garden peas
½ tsp mild curry powder
2 shallots, finely chopped
Oil for frying
Salt and pepper to taste
Balsamic glaze

To make the Scotch eggs

1 Add the white wine vinegar to a large pan of water and bring to the boil.
2 Whisk rapidly to create a whirlpool and carefully place the eggs in the water while it's spinning. Poach for 3 minutes. Remove and drain well.
3 Cut the smoked salmon into strips and wrap two layers around each egg, ensuring it is covered completely.
4 Flour the eggs, pass through the beaten egg, then roll in the breadcrumbs. Repeat the process to gain a good thick covering. When all the eggs are breaded set aside.
5 When you are ready to serve, place the Scotch eggs in a deep fryer and cook until golden brown.

To make the salad

1 Fry the shallots with the curry powder, then add the mackerel, rice and peas.
2 Toss the mixed leaves with the warm mixture.

To serve

Divide the salad between four plates. Place a Scotch egg on top of each and drizzle with a little balsamic glaze.

"Cornish duck eggs are a favourite ingredient of mine, as they have an indulgent texture and taste."

Matthew Rowe, Head Chef and Landlord,
The Falmouth Packet Inn, Rosudgeon, near Penzance

"I was inspired to create this recipe as a new twist on a previous dish of mine. It is important not to overcook the eggs when poaching them. Cornish duck eggs are a favourite ingredient of mine, as they have an indulgent texture and taste.

The best part of my job is having a full dining room with happy food lovers. The worst part is missing out on family and friends time. Another highlight was when my food was compared to Tom Kerridge's. My proudest moment was when we won Gold in the Taste of the West Awards for the first time in 2013.

I like to unwind by either playing golf, or eating a good meal with my family, or walking the dog on the beach."

Boscastle Farm Shop's sweet potato, spinach and brie frittata

Recipe by Will Sherry, Chef, Boscastle Farm Shop, Boscastle

Ingredients

2 large sweet potatoes
12 large free-range eggs
140ml double cream
125g spinach
1 large white onion, diced
6 thick slices of Cornish brie
340g mature cheddar cheese
8 new potatoes
Extra-virgin olive oil
Sea salt and ground black pepper

Method

1 Peel the sweet potatoes, wash and chop them into small pieces.

2 Drizzle the potatoes with the olive oil and roast in the oven for 30 minutes at 180°C/gas mark 4.

3 Meanwhile, boil the new potatoes for 15-20 minutes, or until cooked. Allow to cool, then cut into quarters.

4 Sweat the onion in a frying pan for a couple of minutes and allow to cool.

5 Line a large flan or quiche case with baking parchment paper. If you don't have either, use a large frying pan. Place the onions, sweet and new potatoes roughly around the case or pan.

6 In a large mixing bowl whisk the eggs and cream and season well.

7 Spread the raw spinach in the case or pan and sprinkle the cheddar over the top. Then in a fan-like shape, place the brie on top of the other ingredients.

8 Gently pour the egg mixture around these ingredients, making sure it does not come over the top.

9 Place in a preheated oven at 180°C/gas mark 4 for 10 minutes, then turn the oven down to 170°C/gas mark 3 and cook for another 25-35 minutes. When cooked, the frittata should be golden brown in appearance and not wobble.

10 Turn out of the case, allow to cool for 10 minutes, then serve with a well-dressed mixed leaf salad.

Double chocolate fudge brownies, using fudge from Buttermilk Confections

Recipe by Zannah Reid, Head Chef, Time Café & Gallery, Probus, near Truro

Ingredients

225g soft dark brown sugar

210g butter

150g plain chocolate (75% cocoa solids)

150g Buttermilk Confections' Luxury All Butter Hand Broken Chocolate Fudge

3 eggs, beaten

50g self-raising flour

50g cocoa powder

½ tsp baking powder

Method

1 Grease and line a 20cm square tin.
2 Melt chocolate in a bowl over some simmering water.
3 Beat the sugar and butter together.
4 Add the eggs slowly, beating in well.
5 Sieve the flour, cocoa and baking powder together and fold into the beaten mixture.
6 Add the melted chocolate and mix.
7 Stir in chocolate fudge and pour into the prepared tin.
8 Cook in a preheated oven at 170°C (fan oven)/gas mark 3 for 20-30 minutes, until set and cooked through.
9 Leave to cool in the tin, then lift out carefully and cut into squares.

Top Tip: Freeze chocolate or fudge when adding pieces of it to a cake mixture. That way the chocolate or fudge stays solid for longer.

Zannah Reid, Head Chef, Time Café & Gallery, Probus, near Truro

"I had tried out a few different dessert recipes using this fudge, before I found that it worked really well in my brownie recipe. The ingredients for the brownies are dark and rich, making the accents of this delicious chocolate fudge really stand out.

The best part of my job is working for myself in my small café. I have created a comfortable, friendly meeting place for regulars and visitors and I use local producers and artisan bakers, making everything else myself.

My most exciting moment was walking into this small café in the area where I had lived and brought up my children, to discover that the owner was closing in 20 minutes — for good. I was in the right place at the right time; it was meant to be."

Tracy McDonnell Goad, Managing Director, Buttermilk Confectionery, Bodmin

"Our company specialises in creating handmade, artisan confectionery using kitchen-cupboard ingredients. This includes treats such as fudge, brittles, honeycomb and Turkish delight. Our award-winning products are available across the UK and even as far away as New Zealand. It is important that we source good-quality local ingredients whenever possible; most of those we use come from Trewithen Dairy in nearby Lostwithiel.

The best and worst parts of my job are being surrounded by the most amazing treats every day — it's just so tempting!

There have been many high points in running the business, from winning awards for our products, and Princess Anne telling us how much she enjoys our fudge, to moving into our new premises owing to growth."

Thank you to the following Taste of the West award winners who made this recipe book possible

Arkell's Brewery
01793 823026
arkells.com

Aroma Coffee House & Kitchen
01297 445914
aromalymeregis.co.uk

The Artisan Malt Vinegar Company
01326 281135
artisanmaltvinegar.co.uk

Beaminster Brasserie at the Bridge House
01308 862200
beaminsterbrasserie.co.uk

Beech Ridge Farm
07921 267372
beechridgefarm.co.uk

Bell & Loxton
01548 562023
bellandloxton.co.uk

Blackacre Farm Eggs
01963 33396
blackacrefarmeggs.com

Bocabar
01458 440558 / 0117 972 8838
bocabar.co.uk

Bramley and Gage
01454 418046
bramleyandgage.co.uk

Brinkworth Dairy
01666 510040
brinkworthdairy.co.uk

Brown Cow Organics
01749 890298
browncoworganics.co.uk

Burrow Farm
01392 461215
burrowfarm.com

Buttermilk Confections
buttermilkconfections.co.uk
01208 814505

Capreolus Fine Foods
01935 83883
capreolusfinefoods.co.uk

The Curry Corner
01242 528449
thecurrycorner.com

Denhay Farms Ltd
01404 548262
denhay.co.uk

Dolphin House Brazzerie
01752 254879
dolphinhousebrazzerie.co.uk

Dorset Farms
01308 868822
dorsetfarms.co.uk

Dukes
01395 513503
dukessidmouth.co.uk

The Eastbury Hotel
01935 813131
theeastburyhotel.co.uk

Falmouth Bay Seafood Café
01872 278884
falmouthbayseafoodcafe.com

Falmouth Packet Inn
01736 762840
falmouthpacketinn.co.uk

The George Inn
01297 489419
georgeinnchideock.co.uk

Glasshouse Restaurant
01793 842800
marshfarmhotel.co.uk

The Grove Inn
01769 580406
thegroveinn.co.uk

Hillside Foods
01392 833630
hillsidefoods.co.uk

The Horn of Plenty
01822 832528
thehornofplenty.co.uk

Hunter's Brewery
01803 873509
huntersbrewery.com

Keen's Cheddar
01963 32286
keenscheddar.co.uk

Kittow's Butchers
01726 814926
kittowsbutchers.co.uk

Langsford's Preserves
01749 841007
langsfords-preserves.co.uk

Martin's Meats
01242 621493
martinsmeats.com

M C Kelly
01363 84545
mckelly.co.uk

New Farm Restaurant
01460 240584
newfarmrestaurant.co.uk

No. 4 Peterville
01872 554245
no4peterville.co.uk

Oliver's Falmouth
01326 218138
oliversfalmouth.com

Olive Tree Restaurant
01225 447928
www.olivetreebath.co.uk

Orange Elephant Ice Cream
01392 833776
tavernersfarm.co.uk

Otterton Mill Café
01395 568521
ottertonmill.com

Perry's Cider
01460 55195
perryscider.co.uk

Pork Heaven from Devon
01398 351568
porkheavenfromdevon.com

Primrose Herd
01209 821408
primroseherd.co.uk

The Riverside Restaurant
01308 422011
thefishrestaurant-westbay.
co.uk

The Royal Oak Inn
01822 852944
royaloakinn.org.uk

The Swan Hotel
01454 625671
swanhotelbristol.com

The Swan Inn
01672 870274
theswanwilton.co.uk

Time Café & Gallery
01726 882371

Trewithen Dairy
01208 872214
trewithendairy.co.uk

Tudor Farmhouse Hotel
01594 833046
tudorfarmhousehotel.co.uk

Victoria Inn
01548 842604
victoriainn-salcombe.co.uk

The Watercress Company
01929 401407
thewatercresscompany.co.uk

Waterhouse Fayre
01769 550504
waterhousefayre.co.uk

The White House
01297 560411
whitehousehotel.com

The White Post
01935 851525
thewhitepost.com

Wiltshire Chilli Farm
01225 790733
justchillies.co.uk

Boscastle Farm Shop & Café
01840 250827
boscastlefarmshop.co.uk

The Lordleaze Hotel
01460 61066
lordleazehotel.com

Lynher Dairies Cheese Company
01872 870789
lynherdairies.co.uk

Truffles Brasserie
01749 812180
trufflesbrasserie.com

Index

Whole grilled plaice, with mussel and saffron butter and croquettes using Primrose Herd's chorizo 156

Cider
Slow-cooked belly of pork with Perry's Cider and a sage and cider gravy 36

Old Spot pork tenderloin with Heavenly Hedgerows Three Fruit Marmalade and a cider sauce 46

Apple and cider rarebit with Langsford's Bread and Butter Pickle 64

Seared Lyme Bay scallops with Burrow Farm Black Pudding, celeriac and apple puree and a cider reduction 128

Coconut
Martin's Meats lamb T-bone and fresh coconut makhani 14

Coppa
Fillet of brill with wild garlic, flageolet beans with guanciale, scallops wrapped in lardo, Capreolus Coppa 78

Roast asparagus wrapped in Capreolus Fine Foods' Coppa from Dorset 82

Cornish yarg
Lynher Dairies' Cornish Yarg, shallot and saffron tart 142

Crab
Pan-fried fillet of Cornish hake with a Lyme Bay crab, saffron, spinach and pea risotto using Keen's Whey Butter, with pea shoots and garlic oil 56

Duck
Beech Ridge Farm duck with orange, sesame seeds, sweet potato and green beans 60

Egg
Asparagus with Blackacre Farm's Waddling Free duck eggs, pancetta and black garlic 50

Local watercress, homemade chorizo, garlic croutons and a poached egg salad 70

Homemade Scotch egg, using sausage from Pork Heaven from Devon 118

Smoked posh Scotch egg with a kedgeree salad 160

Boscastle Farm Shop's sweet potato, spinach and brie frittata 164

Fudge
Double chocolate fudge brownies, using fudge from Buttermilk Confections 166

Gin
Elderflower and Bramley & Gage 6 o'clock Gin panna cotta, lemon sorbet and ginger crumb 10

Guanciale
Fillet of brill with wild garlic, flageolet beans with guanciale, scallops wrapped in lardo, Capreolus Fine Foods' Capreolus Coppa 78

Toasted brioche with smoked mutton, wild garlic and Francis cheese 80

Hake
Pan-fried fillet of Cornish hake with a Lyme Bay crab, saffron, spinach and pea risotto using Keen's Whey Butter, with pea shoots and garlic oil 56

Ham hock
Ham hock and Kittow's Butchers' Cornish Hogs Pudding terrine 138

Hogs Pudding
Ham hock and Kittow's Butchers' Cornish Hogs Pudding terrine 138

Houmous
Cumin and Coriander Olive fougasse bread, Olive oil and Red Chilli Harissa houmous 90

Continued on page 174...

Lamb

Martin's Meats lamb T-bone and fresh coconut
makhani 14

Mackerel

Smoked mackerel pâté 88

Cornish mackerel, baby beets, watercress and
crispy shallots with Trewithen Dairy yogurt 152

Smoked posh Scotch egg with a kedgeree salad
160

Mushroom

Beech Ridge Farm free-range chicken,
mushroom and bacon hotpot gratin 44

Mussels

Whole grilled plaice, with mussel and saffron
butter and croquettes using Primrose Herd's
chorizo 156

Mutton

Toasted brioche with smoked mutton, wild garlic
and Francis cheese 80

Nectarine

Arkell's Bee's Organic Ale & honey-poached
nectarines, filled with a sweet cinnamon
mascarpone 24

Olives

Cumin and Coriander Olive fougasse bread,
Olive oil and Red Chilli Harissa houmous 90

Orange

Beech Ridge Farm duck with orange, sesame
seeds, sweet potato and green beans 60

Pear

Royal Bassett Blue cheese beignets, caramelised
pear, walnut pastry, petit salad, sweet and sour
dressing 20

Roasted, marinated loin of venison from
M C Kelly, with pears, juniper and red
cabbage 122

Plaice

Whole grilled plaice, with mussel and saffron
butter and croquettes using Primrose Herd's
chorizo 156

Pork

Slow-cooked belly of pork with Perry's Cider and
a sage and cider gravy 36

Old Spot pork tenderloin with Heavenly
Hedgerows Three Fruit Marmalade and a
cider sauce 46

Double-baked pressed pork belly, using Bell &
Loxton Cold Pressed Rapeseed Oil 104

Outdoor-reared local pork belly cooked in
Hunter's Crispy Pig beer 108

Rice

Brown Cow Organic Vanilla Yoghurt & cardamom
caramelised rice pudding with spiced rhubarb
compote 40

Pan-fried fillet of Cornish hake with a Lyme Bay
crab, saffron, spinach and pea risotto using
Keen's Whey Butter, with pea shoots and garlic
oil 56

The smoked posh Scotch egg with a kedgeree
salad 160

Rhubarb

Brown Cow Organic Vanilla Yoghurt & cardamom
caramelised rice pudding with spiced rhubarb
compote 40

Sea Bass

Fillet of sea bass, with a celeriac and wasabi
remoulade, potato terrine, asparagus and a
lemon and lime mayonnaise 74

Salmon

Wiltshire Chilli Farm Chipotle Chilli Salt gravadlax
30

Smoked posh Scotch egg with a kedgeree salad
160

Scallops

Fillet of brill with wild garlic, flageolet beans with guanciale, scallops wrapped in lardo, Capreolus Fine Foods' Capreolus Coppa 78

Seared scallops, with an avocado rillette and sauce vierge, using Dorset Farms' Honey Smoked Streaky Bacon 94

Seared Lyme Bay scallops with Burrow Farm Black Pudding, celeriac and apple puree and a cider reduction 128

Crispy Cornish Scallops with Artisan Malt Vinegar 148

Sorbet

Elderflower and Bramley & Gage 6 o'clock Gin panna cotta, lemon sorbet and ginger crumb 10

Vanilla cheesecake with an almond tuille and Orange Elephant Pink Grapefruit Sorbet 126

Smoked Cheese

Smoked cheese and toasted seed croquettes with Hillside's Pear, Apple & Herb Chutney 132

Spinach

Boscastle Farm Shop's sweet potato, spinach and brie frittata 164

Yoghurt

Brown Cow Organic Vanilla Yoghurt & cardamom caramelised rice pudding with spiced rhubarb compote 40

Cornish mackerel, baby beets, watercress and crispy shallots with Trewithen Dairy yoghurt 152

Venison

Roasted, marinated loin of venison from M C Kelly, with pears, juniper and red cabbage 122

Watercress

Local watercress, homemade chorizo, garlic croutons and a poached egg salad 70

Cornish mackerel, baby beets, watercress and crispy shallots with Trewithen Dairy yoghurt 152

Vanilla

Vanilla cheesecake with an almond tuille and Orange Elephant Pink Grapefruit Sorbet 126

Wasabi

Fillet of sea bass, with a celeriac and wasabi remoulade, potato terrine, asparagus and a lemon and lime mayonnaise 74

Whey Butter

Pan-fried fillet of Cornish hake with a Lyme Bay crab, saffron, spinach and pea risotto using Keen's Whey Butter, with pea shoots and garlic oil 56